REV. R. H. GRAVES, D. D.

Forty Years in China

OR

CHINA IN TRANSITION

BY

REV. R. H. GRAVES, D.D.

ILLUSTRATED

Scholarly Resources Inc.
Wilmington, Delaware

SCHOLARLY RESOURCES, INC.
1508 Pennsylvania Avenue
Wilmington, Delaware 19806

Reprint edition published in 1972
First published in 1895 by R. H. Woodward, Baltimore

Library of Congress Catalog Card Number: 72-79822
ISBN: 0-8420-1372-5

Manufactured in the United States of America

CONTENTS.

LIST OF ILLUSTRATIONS.

PREFACE.

Tennyson says:

"Better fifty years of Europe than a Cycle of Cathay";
of course he used the word Cycle for an indefinitely long period of time. A "Cycle of Cathay" is really sixty years. So there is not much difference in the two periods after all. The Chinese, governed by their theory of "Heavenly Stems and Earthly Branches," suppose that things run their course, and go through their changes in a period of sixty years. The last sixty years have seen changes in China unprecedented in her history. Nor is it necessary to go back even so far as that; the last forty years have seen China in a stage of transition. During the period of forty years in which my lot has been cast in China, I have been a personal witness to most of these changes.

In a paper on the Changed Relations of China, presented to the Shanghai Conference by Dr. Y. J. Allen, he mentions the treaty of 1861, as the time when China's new relations to the Western world began. The latest book I have seen on the Chinese,

5

" The Real Chinaman," by Chester Holcomb, for some time U. S. Secretary of Legation at Peking, mentions the Tientsin treaty of 1861, as the new era, in which foreigners began to be acquainted with China, and the Chinese with foreigners, and remarks that almost all the changes which have taken place in China have occurred ,within little more then thirty years.

As I came to China in 1856, five years before these changes began, I had an opportunity of seeing tne old state of things, and of watching the progress of " China in Transition." Thus I have undertaken to give a slight sketch of old China, of the Conservative Influences at work tending to fasten upon her the chain of the past, and the Reconstructive Powers which are at work, effecting changes, already marked, and destined in the future to be more marked, and even remarkable.

So this little volume is not one of personal reminiscences of events in my personal history, so much as observations of passing events, and reflections on their tendency toward the great event to which we look forward with hope, and to the consummation of which I have devoted my life, the regeneration of China.

Written at intervals during a brief period of rest in America, and yet a time when I have been subject to frequent calls of duty, I am conscious

that it is full of imperfections. Yet I have tried to
be fair. Endeavoring to speak the truth frankly
as it appears to me, I have tried

> " Nothing to extenuate ;
> Nor set down aught in malice."

I am fully persuaded that the Chinese have many
admirable qualities; qualities that have made, and
are destined still to make them a great nation.
Yet I would be a false friend to that people to
whose elevation I have consecrated my life, and of
whom I have so much hope in the future, were I
not to speak plainly of the influences that are
hurrying them on to ruin unless speedily checked
by their acceptance of progress from the West, and
that Divine religion, which, though originating in
the East, is now propagated from the West.

Hoping that God's blessing may rest upon this
slight tribute toward promoting His truth, I commit
it to the public, hoping it may throw some light
upon the new Eastern question.

R. H. G.

FORTY YEARS IN CHINA.

CHAPTER I.

INTRODUCTORY.

CHINA deserves the attention of all intelligent students of the human race. Its geography and its history, the manners and customs of its people are but partially known to the great majority of our people, while the changes that are taking place there have almost entirely escaped the notice of all except those who are living there, and observing them from year to year.

The name China is derived from the house of *Tsin* or *Ch'in*, a powerful family in Northwest China. The Chow dynasty under which Confucius flourished (b. B. C. 551 : died 478), lasted from B. C. 1100 to 250. In its period of decadence, during which the great Chinese sages, Confucius and Mencius lived, and in the period of the " warring states " which succeeded, the great house of Tsin was lreaded by the rest of China. In B. C. 220, the

prince of this house, Shih Hwang, made himself
Emperor of China, and made the empire one. He
destroyed the ancient books to blot out all remem-
brance of former sovereigns, and built the Great
Wall, 250 miles long, to keep out the Tartar tribes
on the North. From this family the Western name
for China was derived. It was known as Sin, Chin,
Sinae, China and Sinim. The latter term is found
in Is. 49: 12. The best commentators are agreed
that it refers to China, lying to the east of Pales-
tine ; the other points of the compass are mentioned,
the south ("from afar") the north and the west.
Though not yet masters of the empire in Isaiah's time
(unless we admit the late date of the latter part of the
prophecies of Isaiah), still Tsin was the most powerful lordly house, and was in that part of China
which would naturally have the most intercourse
with Western Asia. The Chinese were also known
as *Seres* (the "silk men"), a name derived from the
Chinese name for silk. Hence *Serica* or Seric garments became the Latin term for silk. In the
Middle Ages, China was known as *Cathay*. This
is derived from the Ki-Tans, or Khi-Tai, another
tribe which ruled in China. Ki-Tai is the name by
which the Chinese are known at the present day
among the Russians, and the people of Central
Asia. It will be remembered in connection with
our own country, that Columbus set out for Cathay

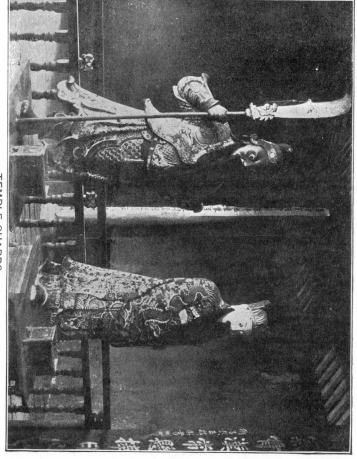

TEMPLE GUARDS.

and Zipangu (Japan) when he discovered America. The Chinese usually call themselves men of *Han*, the dynasty which succeeded Tsin ; or men of *Tang* (A. D. 620).

China, as to its physical geography, is divided into three great divisions, corresponding roughly to those of our own country, except that their divisions run east and west, while ours run north and south. In the center is the great valley of the Yang-Tze, corresponding to our Mississippi basin; while in the north separated from this by the Pei Ling range, is the plain drained by the Yellow River, and in the south, separated by the Mei Ling range, is the section drained by the West River, or *Si-Kiang*, and other streams ; these may be compared to our Atlantic and Pacific slopes. Though lying somewhat further south than the United States, it embraces the same variety of climate and of soil. Its agricultural resources have been utilized for centuries, but its mineral resources are to a great extent undeveloped. Of late years foreign machinery has been introduced and the coal mines of Formosa, and at Kai Peng, near the gulf of Pechili, have been worked successfully. Almost every variety of fruit and of cereals is found in China. Rice is the chief food of the people, and is produced in large quantities in the fertile plains and rich river deltas. In South China two crops a year are raised from

the same soil. Wheat and millet furnish much
of the food for the inhabitants of North China.
Cotton is raised in some places, while, from of old,
silk culture has been one of the chief industries of
the people. The fiber of a species of nettle (*Bœr-
meria*) furnished the grass cloth, and a species of
pandanus the aloe cloth, which are produced in
some parts of China. Tea, of course, is one of the
chief vegetable productions of the empire. It is
the dried leaf of a species of camellia (*Thea Sinen-
sis, Linn.*), and is exported to all parts of the world.
Silk fabrics, China ware, and straw matting are also
among the chief exports from China.

The population of China has been variously estimated. Early in the present century (1807) the official
census gave 360,000,000. Most authorities put it
now at some 400,000,000. Some, however, impressed with the devastation caused by the Tai Peng
rebellion in the Yang-Tze basin, are inclined to put
the population at a lower figure. I think we may
safely take 350 to 360 millions as a sober estimate.
It seems to have increased largely during the present
Dynasty (since 1618). Though much of the
mountain land is still in forest and not occupied by
man, the fertile valleys and extended plains are
very thickly settled, so that China's population to
the square mile is very great. The most populous
city is probably Canton, with a million and a half

inhabitants, then comes Peking, the capital, and other seaports and centers of population, as Shanghai, Foochow, Han-kow, etc.

Semi-historical China goes back as far as B. C. 2249, at which date astronomical observations recorded in Chinese annals have been verified by modern calculations. It has been governed by different families of Chinese, as well as by different Tartar tribes, as the Mongols in 1269 under Kublai Khan and the Manchus (1618) under the present reigning family. Foreign intercourse has extended through many centuries with many interruptions. Traders from the west visited Canton by sea in the thirteenth century, as recorded by Arabian historians, so that foreign influence has made itself felt there for 600 years. An uncle of Mahomet is buried in a mosque just outside the north gate of Canton. The Arabs once captured the city, and a mosque and tower for the muezzin are still standing within the walls of Canton City. The Nestorians came to North China overland in A. D. 635. European intercourse began later. Marco Polo, the Venetian, returned from China in 1274, and his vivid account of the splendid civilization of China and Japan created much interest in these Eastern lands. The Portuguese navigator, Perestello, arrived by sea in the Canton River in 1516. Queen Elizabeth of England attempted to open up commercial inter-

course with China in 1596, but was unsuccessful.
Again attempts were made in 1637, when the
English bombarded the forts in the Canton River.
Trade was begun at Ningpo, Formosa, and Amoy
as well as at Canton.   In modern times commerce
was confined to Canton and the Portuguese colony
of Macao, 90 miles distant on the sea-coast.   Then
came the opening of the five ports of Canton, Amoy,
Foochow, Ningpo, and Shanghai after the " Opium
War " of 1842.

CHAPTER II.

THE OLD AND THE NEW.

CHINA has been a fruitful field for investigation by Western travelers and writers, and many books have been written describing its scenery, its resources, its people and its customs. Many of these are the production of travelers who have given their impressions gained from a hasty observation or statements derived from ignorant and conceited native guides, or from prejudiced foreign residents, while others are the works of men who have spent years among the Chinese, studying their characteristics and patiently investigating their language, history, manners and customs. Some statements made with with regard to China and the Chinese are misleading : for while they may be true of some parts of China, they are not so with regard to others.

China is to be compared to Europe rather than to France or Spain or any other state in Europe, for it is an assemblage of people differing in their language, habits, and customs. While united by their adhesion to the Imperial rule and their reverence for the Confucian classics, they are divided

2

as to many of their ancestral traditions, geographical and climatic environment, local attachments and provincial customs. In reading a book on China we must beware of making any hasty generalizations, and always take into consideration the local standpoint of the writer, and the people by whom he is surrounded. As I have been for many years a resident of South China, of course any remarks I may make are based mainly upon my observation of the people in Canton and its vicinity. Still, the Chinese are in most respects one people, and there are Chinese traits of character as distinguished from that of the European, Japanese or Malay. Just as there is a unity in Christendom based on the fact that our civilization is founded on a common respect for the Bible and the acceptance of certain principles of international law, so there is a unity among the Chinese founded on the fact that for centuries they have accepted the Confucian classics as their standard of morality and civil government, and have been for 2000 years, theoretically at least, under the sway of a common Emperor.

China of to-day is the resultant of these centripetal and centrifugal forces. Its government consists of two elements : the Imperial authority, as represented by Mandarins, high and low, with the underlings and police runners connected with the various official courts, and the popular will represented by the village elders, the *Kung-Kuk,* or councils of literati, and the *Kai-fong* or assemblages of householders in cities and towns. Public opinion, which is, perhaps, practically the strongest element in Chinese society, is based on local traditions, clan-feeling and provincial pride, modified by a sense of nationality founded on allegiance to the Emperor as the Son of Heaven or Divinely-sent Ruler. The Chinese ideas of government are somewhat like those of Louis Napoleon, an Imperialism founded on the will of the people. While the Emperor is supreme, an autocrat sent by Heaven, he must reign for the good of the people; a soon as he manifestly loses the benediction of Heaven by continued reverses, or his reign becomes an injury rather than a blessing to his people, he forfeits his claim to their allegiance. The Chinese theory is illustrated by a popular proverb: "The Emperor's messenger must not disturb a man at his meals." It is this assertion of personal rights, united to a reverence for the Imperial authority, that has made the Chinese the stalwart, law-abiding people that they are.

No one can understand China who regards its government as a pure despotism—an Autocrat imposing his own will on subservient subjects. The popular element must also be taken into consideration in estimating the forces which bind Chinese society together.

In speaking of the government of China we must take into the account another fact, viz. that the Emperor and the people belong to two different races ; speaking entirely different languages—not different dialects merely, as the inhabitants of various parts of China proper—having different traditions and customs. The Manchu Tartars who have governed China for the last 250 years are descended from a nomadic race of horsemen who gloried in their military prowess, while the Chinese are a race of agriculturists and tradesmen who boast of their literature and refinement as compared with their neighbors. The more warlike race has maintained its supremacy over the more numerous and more civilized one, not by mere force of arms, but by wise concessions and a discreet division of power. As the military Romans were molded by the more refined and cultivated Greeks, so the rough Manchus have been influenced by the civilization and literature of the Chinese. They have imitated the Romans too in calling to their aid the ablest men among the conquered race to help in the administration of government. The Vice-royalties and highest offices in the gift of the Emperor are held as often (or oftener) by Chinese as by Manchus. Their theory is that talent and loyalty should rule. Thus the Manchus' rule, though that of an alien race, does not press heavily upon the Chinese nor

HILLS COVERED WITH GRAVES.

wound their self-esteem. Though the glove may be steel it is lined with velvet. Resistance to authority is put down with barbarous severity, but in ordinary times the yoke is not a heavy one. While some few privileges are granted to the ruling race, few hardships are imposed on the subject one. Thus the Manchu rule, though not so beneficent as that of the British in India, is submitted to with equal or even greater willingness by the masses of the people. Under the present Manchu dynasty, commerce has been extended, population has increased (except, perhaps, in those sections overrun by the Tai-Peng rebellion, which was an effort of the Chinese to throw off the Tartar yoke), and the taxes imposed upon the people have not been oppressive.

There are two more forces which we must take into consideration in studying the China of to-day. These are the *Old* and the *New.* The struggle between the conservatism which clings to the Past, and the Spirit of Progress which prompts China to yield to the impulse of modern Western improvement, is a most interesting subject for study. This is perhaps the greatest problem that has ever confronted China in all her long history. All her efforts to shirk it must prove unavailing. Unless her people and rulers have the resolution to face it boldly and settle it wisely, ruin and disintegration will stare them in the face. It is especially to the study of this problem that I now wish to invite attention. Let us notice some of the Sources of China's intense and colossal conservatism, some of the Elements of Destruction and Disintegration which are already at work tending to destroy the prosperity of the past, and some of the New Forces from which we may hope for Reconstruction and Prosperity in the future.

CHAPTER III.

CHINA AT PRESENT.

An intelligent Chinaman recently went with me to the Metropolitan Museum in Central Park, New York. As we examined the remains of antiquity found in the Egyptian and Assyrian departments there, he was struck with the similarity between the customs and utensils of those ancient empires and those of China to-day, and exclaimed, " China to-day is just where these ancient countries were centuries before Christ! " This is true. As Russia is a piece of Asia, transferred to Europe, so China is a piece of Egypt or Babylonia set in the nineteenth century. These ancient lands had a species of civilization equaling, in some respects, that of the modern Occidentals, and yet, in many others, coming far short of it. As the influences of Western Europe have affected modern Russia, so the effect of Western intercourse is beginning to be felt on the China of to-day. Though this influence is increasing, as yet it is but slight. It is still but in germ rather than in fruition.

If you were to go to Canton, one of the largest,

and in some respects one of the most progressive of the native cities of the Empire, you would be struck with the difference between it and any Western city. The narrow streets are filled with low shops with open front and roofs inclining to the street, so that the heavy rains send a stream from the overhanging eaves on the heads of those who pass by; the high brick city walls are surmounted with battlements from whose embrasures peer the mouths of old iron cannon, often without gun-carriages ; the gates, encased in iron, are closed at dusk and opened at daylight. The little shrines at each house and shop-door, where incense is burnt morning and evening to the gods of the soil, remind us of Pompei, with the shrines to the Lares and Penates, rather than of a modern city. The numerous temples, gorgeous with carving of vermilion and gold, and filled with images of their deities, call our attention to the fact that we are in a land of idolaters. The half-clad coolies, often with little more than a loin-cloth, sweating and toiling under their heavy loads, show us that we are in a land where a man is often little more than a beast of burden.

Yet if you enter the neat, well-arranged shops, you will be welcomed with politeness and attention by the well-dressed, smiling shopkeeper; on the street, you will meet many gentlemen dressed in long robes of delicate-colored silk or spotless white grass-cloth.

A general spirit of good-humor, of patient industry, and of unremitting toil characterizes the masses. Though the bustling coolies, as they jostle against one another in the crowded streets, sometimes give went to their feelings in cursing and quarreling, yet, on the whole, they are ready to beg pardon for any unintentional collision and to grant it without delay. Fights are rare, much fewer than they would be among Western laborers in similar circumstances.

A walk through the narrow streets—or rather alleys as we would call them, for many are not wider than our sidewalks—would show a sight unusual to Western eyes. In the early evening the fragrant smoke of the incense arises from the door-shrines; each place of business has its lantern hanging at the door inscribed with the name of the shop, while in the middle of the street, above the heads of the passers-by, is hung a peanut-oil lamp. In most of the open shops this oil has given way to American or Russian kerosene. In a few streets electric lights are found, but the introduction of electricity has hardly proved a success. Not only are the city gates closed at night, but at the end of each block is a barrier of perpendicular wooden bars or of wooden gates swung on hinges. After 8:30 or 9, P. M. in the winter and 11 in the summer, these barriers are closed, so that no one can pass until he can arouse the watchman or wait for him until he

makes his next round.　These barriers afford great
security against robbery, for if the watchmen are
faithful the robbers have little chance of escape.
Besides these street watchmen, there are others
who in the winter time go their rounds on a plank
pathway constructed on the tops of the houses, or
look out for fires from high watch-towers built of
bamboo.

If one goes inside the dwelling-houses, he will
find little to correspond with our ideas of a *home*.
Comfort and cleanliness are generally wanting.
Luxurious seats and spring-beds are not to be found.
White curtains, graceful hangings and soft carpets
are all conspicuous by their absence.　The floors
are paved with porous tiles, or, in the poorer houses,
are simply hard-beaten earth.　Yet in the houses of
the wealthy there is no little elegance.　The stiff-
backed chairs and tables are of carved ebony or in-
laid with mother-of-pearl or marble.　The divan is
supplied with mats and cushions on which the
guests may recline and smoke their opium, while
they may sip their tea and take their refresh-
ments from choice china on the little marble-
topped teatrays or tables arranged around the
room.

Here and there along the family streets are found
the school-rooms where the boys store their memories with Confucian lore, and learn to write the

complicated but expressive characters of the Chinese language. The girls are not sent to school.

On the river a lively scene presents itself to the eye. Boats of all sizes are made fast along the banks or anchored in mid-stream, while the little *sampans*, or boats for carrying private passengers, flit to and fro, like water-spiders on the surface of a still stream. In some parts, the river is blocked up with the "flower boats," inhabited by loose women, and as gorgeous as a gilded saloon, with carvings, stained-glass windows and splendid mirrors. In others are lines of cargo-boats with their loads of merchandise. At their wharves or buoys are the public passenger-boats with their huge sails, and steerage and decks crowded with passengers. Many of them are fitted with stern wheels, which are propelled by a dozen or more of men working on a tread-mill; for with their tendency to adopt and adapt, the Chinese have taken the model of our American stern-wheelers on our western rivers and arranged the wheel to work by man-power instead of by steam. Others of these passage-boats are towed by the little steam-tugs which abound on the river. In mid-stream are anchored the Chinese steam gun-boats and men-of-war built in Europe or at the Chinese dock-yards. Then, running rapidly with the current, or laboring against a head tide, may be seen the old style police-boats propelled by banks of oars like the ancient triremes.   The steamers and the stern-wheelers are a result of Western progress infringing against the customs of old China, and have been in use only during the last twenty-five years.

Waterways are the great means of intercommunication in China.   The largest cities and towns are usually on the river-side.   Canals have been used in China from time immemorial, and the Grand Canal, about 1000 miles long, constructed in the thirteenth century, is one of the best known engineering works in the world.   When the rivers have a slight fall and are too shallow even for the small, flat-bottomed boats, they are frequently made navigable by low dams, with a narrow outlet forming a slight rapid, up which the boats are forced by poling and by tow-lines.

The Chinese passage-boats are as far removed as possible from the elegance and comfort of our Fall River or Chesapeake Bay steamers.   The passengers are crowded into a steerage saloon too low for one to stand erect in, where each man spreads his mat on the hard floor and is satisfied with a space three feet wide, and glad if he can find room to stretch out his legs.   Men who wish to go short distances can take as a private conveyance a *sampan* or a slipper-boat with as much room as in a cab.   Those who have the means can hire pleasant and roomy boats for $1.50 to $3.00 a day.

As to manufactures, the rude results of Chinese handicraft will generally bear no comparison with the finished products of Western machinery. Yet you will find some very beautiful and artistic fabrics as the outcome of very primitive and rude looms, and fine brohzes, jewels, filigree work, chinaware, lacquer and embroidery produced by Chinese artisans. In the western suburbs of Canton you may enter a small, dirty room, with a floor of earth, and find there men working on a loom of the rudest construction, and see to your surprise the most gorgeous brocades and soft silks and gauzes of the most delicate shades of pink and lilac, woven in graceful patterns, issuing from the loom. A half-naked man mounted on top of the simple loom produces the most elaborate figures by shifting a series of bamboo rods. The Chinese have certainly succeeded in producing some of the most highly finished products with the simplest machinery. The Chinese, like the ancients, cut and polish the hardest gems into any shape they may wish.

Most of their manufactures are so in truth, for they are really the work of men's *hands*. Machinery is comparatively rare. Nor is it especially desired. For the greatest good to the greatest number is the maxim by which the Chinese go, and the great problem is to provide occupation and procure food for as many men as possible. Hence labor-saving machinery is not thought desirable, as it would throw so many men out of employment and add them to the " dangerous classes " which are a source of disorder and weakness in the state. Hence we see in China few of the sad results which monopoly and machinery have produced in the West.

If you go into the country you will find the people, not living in scattered farm-houses as our farmers do, but in villages. These villages are protected by gates which are closed by night and are often surmounted by a watch-tower. This shows the existence of a feeling of insecurity, so that men have to live in barricaded villages for mutual protection from robbers. It is also possible because the holdings of the farmers are but small, resembling garden-patches rather than our large farms and plantations.

The Chinese system of land-tenure has resulted in a large number of freeholders owning a few acres of land apiece rather than in wealthy land-lords holding a monopoly of the soil. They have thus escaped many of the difficulties which have produced so much dissatisfaction with landlordism and land monopoly in Europe and America. If a large body of yeoman freeholders be the backbone of the state, the Chinese have gone far towards securing such a source of strength.

The clan-system is the basis of Chinese society.

The villages are generally inhabited by the same clan and are frequently known by the clan name, as we might have Smithville or Jonesboro called from the original settler, only that in China it would be inhabited by his descendants. Sometimes a village will have two or three clans residing in it, especially if it be a large one. The lands are the property of the members of the clan, and cannot be alienated to men of other clan-names, though they may be freely sold to members of the same clan. Thus the men of each village, being descended from a common ancestor, and growing up under certain family traditions, and surrounded by the same influences for generations, often have a character of their own. Some villages have the name of being mild and polite, others rough and quarrelsome, others proud and overbearing. While custom ordains (and nothing is stronger than custom in China) that the mother must be from a different clan from the father, yet, being from various families, the hereditary traits and taints follow those of the paternal ancestors. This ancestral pride is strengthened by the fact that each village has its ancestral temple where the tablets of the ancestors are placed and their spirits are worshiped. Here the clan assembles, and, with the spirits of their forefathers, as they imagine, looking down upon them and still taking an interest in family affairs, they consult

3

with regard to the interests of the family. To be excluded from the clan is a punishment equal to that of excommunication among the Jews or among the Christians of the Middle Ages.

Besides these villages there are market-towns scattered throughout the country. These contain stores or shops, and the covered market-houses and open spaces where the country people bring their produce on market-days. These days occur on fixed dates two or three times during each ten days, thus on the 3d, 6th, 9th, 13th, 16th, 19th, etc., of each month. Another town 12 or 15 miles distant might have its market-days on the 4th, 7th, 10th, etc. Thus the country people from the surrounding villages take their produce up to the market-towns for sale, and make their purchases from the storekeepers or the hawkers and hucksters who frequent these fairs. On the next day these men carry their wares to the next town. The larger towns always have one or more pawnbrokers' shops, and these high buildings, towering above the surrounding houses, form quite a marked feature in the landscape as we travel in China.

The houses in the country villages are usually of adobe or sun-dried brick and of concrete. Some of the poorer sort are of bamboo wattles, coated with mud, while those of the better class are of burnt brick.

The Chinese are satisfied with their simple country houses, for they know no better. To us the general impression is that of squalor and poverty ; yet many of their purest pleasures and most pleasing memories cluster around the homes of their childhood, and they show as sincere an attachment to their ancestral villages and temples, as men of more favored lands feel towards their more comfortable and elegant dwellings on country farms.

This chapter may afford a glimpse of China, or at least of South China, as it is to-day. Of course there are many other things which might well claim our attention, but time does not allow us to describe them.

CHAPTER IV.

CHINA'S CONSERVATISM.

To the Western mind, the most striking characteristic of the Chinese is their intense, colossal conservativism.   National pride is a trait of all strong nations who have anything to be proud of.   While, to a certain extent, an element of strength, it is very apt to degenerate into mere senseless boasting.   All stalwart people have virtues of which they may well be proud, generally mingled with traits of character of which the more thoughtful are ashamed.   No one nation has a monopoly of all the virtues.   However eager a blind patriotism may be to claim this, a man with a cosmopolitan mind can see faults as well as virtues in all.   But men of narrow minds, filled with utter ignorance of other lands, as most of the Chinese are, are inclined to think that all excellences belong to their own race.   The same reason which led the ancient Greeks to look down on other nations who were their inferiors in art, culture, and civilization as *barbarians*, leads the Chinese to despise other peoples. At one time the Chinese were superior to the surrounding tribes in many things.   These notions have become imbedded in their literature, and so ignorant are they of the fact that the world has made progress during the centuries and that other nations exist that are superior to Tartars and Siamese, that they still look upon this land as the " Central Kingdom " and all other men as " outside barbarians." They are as firmly persuaded that the Emperor of China is the rightful " Universal Sovereign " as Roman Catholics are that the Pope is the rightful head of the universal church. I have heard Chinese, in other respects intelligent, speak of the war of the English against China as " rebellion," and foreigners who oppose the will of the Emperor, as " rebels." Whatever may be their acknowledgment of the fact that there are *de facto* governments in the world, they feel that there can be but one *de jure* Emperor, the Vicegerent of Heaven upon earth, and that the Emperor of China is the man.

Just as the Jews consider themselves the only depositories of the Divine Revelation, so the Chinese think that they—" the black-haired race "—are the depositories of the heavenly truths transmitted through the ancient sages, and so are the superiors of all other men. The Chinese are the model race, to whom all others must look up with deference. An amusing illustration of this innate feeling occurred in one of the mission schools in Canton. The teacher was questioning the boys about the characteristic colors of the various races of mankind, and asked, " What is the color of the Chinese ? " a boy at once called out, " Human color." While this self-conceit is not peculiar to the Chinese by any means, yet it is very marked among them, and perhaps more intense than in most peoples. Nor is the reason for this trait difficult to understand. Isolated from more cultivated nations, preserving or developing a civilization along her own lines, looked up to by her neighbors, she soon learned to arrogate to herself a position of superiority which was readily accorded by the adjoining nations. Even though they might claim superiority in martial prowess, they granted that China was their superior in literature and civilization. Thus Japan, Tartary, Thibet, and Anam received much of their civilization and literature from China, and fully acknowledged their dependence on her.

It is not strange that a people whose self-conceit is so marked should cling to the traditions of the past and be slow to yield the palm of superiority to any other nation.

Some one may say, But it is impossible that they should not see the superiority of Western nations in the war vessels which visit their ports, their improved armaments and drill, the superior comfort and luxury in the residences of the foreign merchants, the excellence of the roads and street-lights and water-works in Hong Kong and Shang-

hai, or that those Chinese who have been in Europe
and America should not acknowledge the proofs of
an advanced civilization which they see there. The
more intelligent Chinese, especially those who have
been abroad, acknowledge these things, but usually
say, Yes, they are ahead of us, but it is only because they have more wealth! If we Chinese were
not so poor we would have all these things too.
Many others say, Yes, but it is only in mere
material civilization, in the display of brute force,
that Western nations excel. When it comes to the
world of thought they cannot compare with our
sages in their knowledge of virtue, to our mystics
in their subtle reveries, to our philosophers in their
profound speculations. Of course this intense self-
conceit is based on profound ignorance. They have
fixed it in their minds as an axiom that the ancient
Chinese sages are the Heaven-sent teachers to teach
mankind virtue and morals and the principles of
political economy. So they deem other literature
as beneath their notice, and would no more think of
learning a foreign tongue to examine for themselves
the writings of Plato or Aristotle, Homer or Virgil,
Moses or Paul, Bacon or Kant than we would
think of deriving any moral or philosophical thought
from the picture-writing of the Aztecs or North
American Indians. Their literati having been trained
for generations to consider the teaching of Chinese

sages and philosophers as the paragon of excellence, feel that it is profanity to compare these men with any barbarian, and resent any attempt to disturb the dream of their self-satisfaction. While one of the sayings ascribed to Confucius is that " Western nations also have their sages," the Chinese feel that any instructions Western sages may have are not for them, but are for the Western men.

Some of the Chinese are confirmed in their notions of Chinese superiority by the fact that Western students have examined and translated the writings of Confucius and other philosophers. Just as some conceited heathen went away from the Parliament of Religions in Chicago with the notion that Americans are getting tired of Christianity and sought them as religious instructors, so these Chinese, unable to comprehend the spirit of investigation which characterizes the Western mind, have jumped at the conclusion that these scholars are trying to introduce Confucianism into Europe. Dr. James Legge, after having spent years as an able Christian missionary in Hong Kong, is now a professor at Oxford, and is spending the evening of his days in translating and publishing the writings of the Chinese sages. From this some Chinese have inferred and asserted that having become convinced that the Chinese do not need Christianity he is now trying to persuade the English to accept Confucianism.

EXAMINATION HALL.—STUDENTS' APARTMENTS.

It is not strange that the Chinese should set a high value on the teachings of Confucius and Mencius and others, and that, knowing nothing better, they should consider them unsurpassable. They really contain much that is excellent, and in many respects may be compared to the book of Proverbs, with God left out. The ethical and political maxims of Confucius contain much valuable morality and wisdom. His conduct, as recorded in the classics, has been the mold into which the Chinese ideals of perfection have been cast. Confucius is an uncrowned king. His teachings have influenced more of the human race than those of any other man, with the exception perhaps of the Lord Jesus Christ. It is not strange that the Chinese, knowing his good points, should be proud that their land has produced such a man, and think that his teachings are unsurpassed. Mencius does not come far below Confucius, and in his straightforwardness his character seems to some foreigners to surpass that of Confucius.

Lao-Tse, the author of the *Tao-Teh-King* and reputed founder of Tauism, reminds us of our own Emerson in his reflections. A German writer, Victor von Strauss, styles him "A prophet among the Gentiles, and gives him a high place among the teachers of the world.*

*See "Miss. Review of the World," vol. viii. p. 95.

Taking all these things into consideration it is not surprising that the Chinese are narrow-minded and self-conceited.

Another cause for the exaggerated conservatism of the Chinese is found in their *veneration for the past* We who have been trained under the influence of the Inductive philosophy and the hopefulness inspired by the Bible, look for constant progress, and for our Golden Age in the future. But to the Chinese, as to the Greeks and Romans, the Golden Age was in the past. The lives of men at the present day come so inexpressibly short of the models laid down and the conditions described as having place in ancient times, that the Chinese suppose perfection is to be attained only by trying to go back to those times. The fact of a degeneration in morals in some lines is probably true, and the primitive simplicity of their ancestors centuries ago was in advance of modern corruption. Having none of the hopes inspired by the Gospel as to the future coming of the Christ and reign of righteousness, it is not singular that they should place their ideal world in the remote past. " The times of Tao and Shun," are the age of perfection to which they look back. Like a man walking backwards, advancing in one direction, while his face is turned toward the other, China has stumbled slowly along the centuries. The glamour of the past has blinded her eyes to the pressing claims of the present and the glorious possibilities of the future. Like an old man, " remembering only the times of his youth," she goes along, irascible and annoyed at the changes that come, and helplessly protesting against the progress of the age. Wringing her trembling hands she sets her aged teeth and exclaims, " *non possumus*," as any advance is pressed upon her. This is the spirit of Chinese Conservatism.

Respect for the aged is a very commendable trait in Chinese character, and one that should be imitated in more favored lands, but they seem to have transferred the respect rightfully due to the individual to the past history of their country. Legends of the past seem to interest Chinese scholars more than plans for the future. This reverence for the past shows itself sometimes in a way that appears ridiculous to foreign eyes. Even the more progressive scholars who wish to advocate some modern improvement find it necessary to cater to the prejudices of the people by claiming that it is only a *restoration* of what was practiced in the past ages. Thus they sacrifice truth in order to secure a reception of their advice by the people. Any one who has heard Chinese music knows what a din of confusion it is. A Chinese musician with a natural ear for the " concourse of sweet sounds," on hearing a piano at once exclaimed, " This is the music our

ancestors lost!" So all the skill of modern surgery
is viewed as only going back to the art of *Wa T'o*,
who could cut a man's head off and sew it on
again! The Chinese are astonished at nothing, but
always profess to be able to match it with something that occurred in China in the past. It will
never do to acknowledge that Western barbarians
can surpass the ancient Chinese in anything. Thus
their self-conceit and exaggerated veneration for
past ages, go hand in hand to confirm the Chinaman
in his conservatism.

Another cause of the conservatism of the Chinese
is the *prevalence of Confucianism* and its intimate
alliance with the State. I have already alluded
to Confucius and his writings, but now wish to
speak of the conservative tendency of his system.
Filial Piety lies at the basis of his whole system.
Dr. Martin, president of the Imperial Tungwen
College of Peking, says: " Confucius lived in an age
when old traditions were being abandoned, when
the bonds of social order were relaxed, and he felt
that he could save society in no other way than by
imposing a check on the spirit of change. In Filial
Piety he found the needed prophylactic. To the
Buddhist, change is hell, and exemption from it
heaven. To the Confucianist, change is vice, and conservatism the first of all virtues. Confucius was a
reformer but not an innovator. Nothing can exceed

the symmetry of the system which he builds on this cardinal virtue (Filial Piety). Extending from parents to remote ancestors, it binds the present to the past, and ramifying in every direction brings the whole of human conduct within the sphere of its sway. So well did he and his disciples recommend it, that every Dynasty has adopted it as the best guarantee for social and political stability." *

Again Dr. Martin says: "The present dynasty professes to govern by Filial Piety, *i-hsiao chih tien-hsia.* Like all that is best in religion and morals, Filial Piety easily degenerates into cant and hypocrisy. If it offers a barrier to revolution, it also opposes changes for the better."

Sir Chaloner Alabaster, a British Consul-General, with years of acquaintance with China and the Chinese, says: "Certainly, as taught and practiced, Filial Piety is productive of good. But where, and in many cases it is so, the measuring of Filial Piety is held to be a slavish reverence for one's grand-fathers, and the practice is confined to a refusal to lepart from their ways, and a strict conformity to the ritual laid down whenever one of your elders dies, the teaching and practice bring the present generation into conflict with the spirit of the time, and must so far be held to be injurious."

Thus what Confucius proposed as a remedy for

* " Chinese Recorder," vol. xxv., No. 10.

the evils of his time has been accepted as the basis of government for all time, just as sometimes in Christendom, creeds which have been adopted as protests against prevailing errors have been taken as complete summaries of all truths to be believed. I do not mean by this that Confucius did not intend his teachings for all ages, or believed that they were merely a remedy for the evils of his own times. The soporific effect of this teaching has been felt all through Chinese society.

Though the connection between Confucianism and the state is very close, it can hardly be called the state religion of China in the sense in which we speak of some of the state religions of Europe. No tithes are levied for its support. No places of public worship are opened which the people are expected to attend. The fact of a man's being a Confucianist does not keep him from holding at the same time, Buddhist or Tauist sentiments, nor prevent his worshiping Buddhist or Tauist idols. Some even of the Chinese emperors have favored Buddhism and others Tauism. The Government of China allows much freedom of religious belief, and does not persecute any religion as such, but only as it may grow suspicious of it as likely to prove injurious to the state. Still, the spirit of Confucianism influences the Government. The state worship of the Emperor and his subordinates is the outcome of this system. Though the Confucian system is one of morals and of political philosophy rather than of religion, still ancestral worship, which is practically *the* religion of the Chinese, is the result of Confucianism. The Chinese have come to identify Filial Piety with the worship of ancestors. Perhaps Confucius is not to be held directly responsible for this, and yet it is the influence which they have not unnaturally derived from his teachings. Ancestral worship, whatever may have been its original significance, as practiced by the great mass of the Chinese to-day goes beyond mere memorial services in honor of one's progenitors, and becomes an actual seeking of blessing from the *manes* of the departed. It peoples the air with spirits, "ascending and descending" who have the the power to confer blessings or inflict punishments on their descendants. Thus it comes into conflict with Christianity, which teaches that one God alone has the power to bless mankind and that prayer should be made to Him only.

The Chinese cling most tenaciously to ancestral worship because they confound it with Filial Piety, which is right and commends itself as such to the natural conscience. Thus it becomes the stronghold of Conservatism.

As education in China is simply memorizing and commenting on the writings of Confucius and

4

the other sages, it has become fossilized. Not only are the classics, or the writings edited or spoken by Confucius and Mencius, the basis of the Government examinations, but the commentary of Chu Fu Tsz is the only authorized exposition of these writings. The Chinese have many commentators with differing views as to many points, but if a student should venture to give an independent view of any passage, differing from that of the Commentator authorized by the Government, he would do so at the risk of his prospects of success. Not only must the writer of the essay use words for which there is ancient authority, which is well enough perhaps, but his essay increases in value as it is filled with quotations from former authors or allusions to them. Everything like independence and freshness is frowned upon. Acquaintance with ancient authors, and elegance and skill in orderly expression of his sentiments is the great thing aimed at in a Chinese scholar. I was traveling once with a student on his way to the Government examination. He was cramming his memory from a book which he let me look at. It consisted of a list of authorized similes which could be used in Government essays, systematically arranged under various heads, e. g. under *red*, the dawn might be compared to a rose, a pink hibiscus, a cherry, etc. If he himself should have happened to think of a

SUMMER HOUSE AND LOTUS POND.

comparison not in the books, and should use it in his essay, it would count as a fault. It may readily be seen what kind of poetry would be the outcome of such a mechanical process of memorizing. In dictating an image to my Chinese writers, I have frequently heard them say: "Nobody will understand that; there is no authority for such a simile." Thus anything like originality is looked on as a defect in writing.

As the Chinese think that the feet of their women are made more beautiful by being cramped and bound, so they seem to consider that the minds of the men must undergo the same process. Minds trained in this mold produce products like our old-fashioned lawns and gardens with stiff rows of Lombardy poplars, and cedars and box trimmed squarely, no room being left for a straggling bough to show its grace or for nature to manifest any of her forms of beauty.

CHAPTER V.

CONSERVATISM—CONTINUED.

THE *Chinese language,* and especially its written forms, tends to confirm the people of China in their conservatism. The written characters possess a beauty of their own, and present a pleasing variety of expression within certain lines. But they do not easily lend themselves to express new ideas. Foreigners, in translating scientific books into Chinese, have constructed technical terms by combining Chinese characters, but I am not aware of any one venturing to write a new character, as no one would understand it. For instance, when chemists called one of the component gases of water, *hydrogen,* it became a part of our language with a definite meaning. It has been called in Chinese, *hing hi,* " the light gas," from its low specific gravity, a very appropriate name, but a Chinaman, seeing it in a book, would not know whether it was a definite substance or merely any gas that was not heavy. Christianity has been in contact with Chinese minds for centuries and it might have been supposed that a word might have been found for our " week." No new character has been invented though a combination of *seven* and *day* might have been easily constructed. The only way to express week is *sih yih ki*, " a period of seven days," which is cumbrous; or *li-pai*, " worship," which was originally, and is still applied to Sunday in *li-pai-yih*, " worship-day," and this is very awkward, as using Sunday for week would be in English. Besides " one worship," i. e. one week, is merely a colloquial expression, and would not be admitted into any book of any value. If there were a National Academy, as in France, it is not probable that they would have the boldness to coin new words to express the new ideas which have resulted from foreign intercourse.

With regard to the spoken language the want of an alphabet prevents the Chinese from expressing foreign sounds. Thus in proper names they can only give an *approximate* imitation of the sounds by using Chinese characters. The nearest they can get to English is *Ying-kee lei*, to France is *Fah-lan-see*, to our president is *pee-lee-see-tin-teh*. The genius of the Chinese language tends to terseness and to shorten long expressions, so they say simply *Ying* for English, *Fah*, for France, etc.

Thus the language, especially in its written form, seems to present a barrier to the introduction of new ideas and new words. This must tend to promote the conservatism of the people. I do not mean that it is impossible to introduce new terms by using combinations of characters already in use, but that the language does not easily and naturally lend itself to such as a permanent addition to the authorized vocabulary. The Chinese language forms a kind of breast-work, not absolutely impregnable perhaps, behind which Conservatism may hide itself from the assaults of progress.

There remains another bulwark of Conservatism in the *number and the ignorance of the people.* The best estimates put the population of the Chinese Empire at about 400 millions of souls. A large mass moves slowly. It is easy to set a little water to boiling in a tea-kettle, while the same amount of heat will make no appreciable elevation of temperature in a large caldron filled with water. None of the heat is lost, but the effects do not appear. So it is with a large mass of men.

Then, there is a great difference in the traits of character of various nations. Just as the melting point of mercury or of lead is comparatively low, while that of iron or of gold is much higher, so some people, as the Latin races of Southern Europe, are excitable and volatile, while others, as the Teutonic races, are more phlegmatic and sturdy. The Chinese resemble the latter rather than the former. They are not an emotional people, but slow, plodding, averse to change and patient and content to endure rather than quick to change. Their natural temperament leads them to conservatism. Had it not been for these staying qualities they would not have maintained their existence as a nation so long. They are not a new people, but can look back upon centuries of civilization before the nations of Europe existed or had emerged from the barbarism of our forefathers. They argue, and not altogether without wisdom, that there is little need of change for a nation which has stood the shocks of centuries. Like some giant oak towering above the surrounding trees and shrubs, they feel that they have a vigorous growth, and their roots are firmly set, and they need make no change. It is not surprising that the Chinese people with their immense numbers, their somewhat phlegmatic natures and their great antiquity should be slow to welcome new ideas.

Another cause of the intense conservatism of the masses of the Chinese, is their dense *ignorance*. China, it is true, has a system of education, but this is exceedingly rudimentary, and fails to give any real enlightenment to the masses of the people. As compared with Americans, the proportion of the Chinese who are educated is very small. In some parts of China most of the boys go to school for two or three years, but in other parts comparatively few have this advantage. Their hours of study are very irregular: in the village schools, as the people are mostly poor, the boys are kept at home during harvest and at other times when their help is required in the fields, or at the home. Notwithstanding these frequent interruptions, many of the pupils study hard and make fair progress in their studies. As they are taught individually and not in classes, they do not lose anything through their absence, but take up their lessons where they left them off. The fact that their education is little more than a mere exercise of *memory* tends to train their minds in conservatism. Their memories and their powers of observation are cultivated by storing their minds with numerous characters, often complicated and nearly resembling one another. While the pupils are in what we might term the primary department, i. e. the first three years of their schooling, they are not taught to think or do any constructive work, nor even taught the *meaning* of the characters; their whole attention is directed to their *form* and their places in the sentences which the pupils commit to memory. Afterwards the teacher begins to explain the meaning of what the scholars have gone over. Of course the pupils understand the meaning of the words in ordinary use, and may have an idea of the gist of many of the sentences they learn, but no direct attempt is made to expound the meaning until they progress further in their studies. The educational training is conducted on the same

lines as that formerly employed in teaching the
catechism to young children; their memories were
charged with deep doctrines and theological terms
which they were not expected to understand until
they were older. In some regards this system may
be a useful one, and if needed anywhere one would
think it would be in learning such a cumbrous
written language as the Chinese is.

My remarks hitherto have had reference simply
to Chinese primary education, which is all that
many of the boys ever receive. Other pupils can
afford to go to school for five or six years and to
obtain advantages which correspond more nearly to
what we understand by an education. They are
taught the meaning of the classics which they have
committed to memory, their wits are exercised in
composing antithetical couplets, and their constructive ability is called out by writing essays. They
are trained to write their complicated characters
with neatness, and to express themselves in writing
with correctness, clearness and rhetorical smooth-
ness. Still all their ideas are formed on ancient
models, and no reaching out toward freshness or
novelty would be tolerated. The great thing is to
be able to quote the ancients with pertinence and
elegance of language. Independent thought or
investigation would meet with no encouragement.
Pupils with this degree of education will be able to

read ordinary books with more or less of intelligence, and to write the usual letters of business or friendship. Most shopkeepers and business men are educated to this extent, and find it sufficient for the common affairs of life.

We come now to the *Government system of education.* This is not intended, like our public school system, to uplift the masses and fit them for the duties and responsibilities of citizenship, but to *select* a body of men who may prove useful to the state. The object of the Government Examinations is to afford an opportunity, by competitive examination, for all who wish to qualify themselves for the civil or military service of the Government. They correspond more nearly to our Civil Service examinations than to our Common-School system. The competition is open to all (with a few exceptions, as play-actors, descendants of criminals, etc.), and those who wish to enter the lists must prepare themselves by a further course of study than that pursued by the trading class. They spend some years under teachers who are themselves graduates, and who train them in the art of composing essays and in the rhetoric and literature of China. The "classics," or ancient writings, are the basis of this study. These students, or "book-readers," as the Chinese term them, form a class by themselves— men who aspire to be rulers and leaders of the

TOMB OF WEALTHY MAN.

people. Those who have become graduates are accorded certain privileges, as liberty of access to the officials, freedom from being chained when arrested, etc., and are much venerated by their fellow clans, men. These graduates often form a kind of municipal or village council (*Kung Kuh*) and sometimes succeed in getting much power into their hands, even occasionally the power of life and death. I remember seeing by the road-side a row of thirty-six heads of offenders executed by the orders of one of these councils. They sometimes keep bodies of soldiers in their pay, and have armed vessels, in order to arrest and punish obnoxious characters. Thus to become one of the literati or " gentry," as they are sometimes called, is the object of the ambition of many an aspiring student. These honors, however, are only by the way. They all aspire to become mandarins or officers of the Imperial Government with rank and emolument, and a prospect of regularly rising in the service. Thus not only do their studies, but their hopes and ambitions, lead them to be conservative. These men, while generally acquainted with the history and literature of their own country, know very little of geography, even of China, and nothing whatever of mathematics, physics, or the history and geography of other nations. When even the best educated are so ignorant, what must the masses be?

This dense mass of ignorance forms an impenetrable jungle through which any ideas of progress find it very difficult to make their way.

When we take into consideration the innate self-conceit of the Chinese, their intense veneration for the past, the retrospective tendency of Confucianism, the fixity of the Chinese language and the gross ignorance of all other nations which characterizes the masses of the people, we can understand somewhat of the strength of the conservatism which holds China fast in its bonds. As the Chinese built the great wall to prevent the ingress of their Tartar neighbors, so now they have surrounded themselves with a great wall of prejudice, suspicion, and conservatism. But, as their wall proved a futile barrier, and they are now governed by the Manchus, one of the tribes whom they hoped to keep out, so their conservatism must yield to the pressure of the spirit of the times and the progressive ideas of the West. Japan was even more exclusive than China, but she was wise enough to accept the inevitable, and so must China be if she wishes to maintain her existence as a nation. In the rush of the nations down the mighty stream of time it is impossible for any one people, however ponderous its weight, however great its resources, however strong its prejudices, however conservative its traditions, to resist the force of the current and the impact of its neighbors. The towering iceberg may have its vast roots deep in the Arctic Seas, but must feel the force of the current, and really, though slowly and sullenly it may be, float southward; it must yield to the increasing influence of warmer water and brighter sunshine until it becomes a part of the surrounding waters and mingles itself with the great ocean. So China cannot forever remain frozen fast to the traditions of the past. She must give way to the powerful clash of other Powers, or yield to the genial influences of an advanced civilization and of a truer and purer Religion.

CHAPTER VI.

DESTRUCTIVE FORCES.

Let us now notice some of the destructive forces which are at work, slowly it may be, but none the less surely, in undermining Chinese Society. Tendencies to decay are found in all states. As in the physical body life is maintained by getting rid of effete and poisonous elements, and supplying their place by new and vigorous particles, so it is in the body politic. Vitality is evinced by sloughing off dead decaying matter and absorbing new. A constant struggle is going on. If the toxic organisms and dead matter gain the mastery, degeneration and death must ensue. So in the state, virile, stalwart nations succumb to the softening influences of luxury and hardening effects of vice. When religion degenerates into formalism, and morality into conventionalism, Society is sick. When sensualism and self-indulgence displace conscientiousness and self-denial, when self-seeking supplants patriotism, and greed, honesty; when deceit and injustice drive out honor and righteousness, then the seeds of decay are germinating and the harvest of ruin is not far distant. These things are true in every land. Still some evil tendencies may be more marked in one land and others in another. I wish to mention some of these which are at work to-day in China.

All lands have not the same standard of virtue and vice. Even in Christian countries there have been different theories as to what constitute virtue and vice. I accept the Bible as a revelation from God, and conformity to God's revealed will as the true standard of virtue. Still we must deal fairly with those peoples who are ignorant of the Script-ures and have no other light than that of the natural conscience. We make righteousness the standard, the Chinese humanity. We say, " Is it right ? " the Chinese, " Is it kindly ? " With us a man insists upon his " rights," and looks upon any infringement of them as a wrong ; in China a man rather considers his circumstances and asks what is to be expected in the case. The Chinese have a proverb, " One leaf is not missed from a big tree," by which they mean that there is no harm in helping yourself to a little of what a rich man owns. He will not suffer from the theft and so no wrong is done. But to steal from the poor is considered a great outrage. We have a practical illustration of this in China. I have seen a little stall of fruit or sweetmeats by the side of the street

with the prices marked on each pile of peanuts or
sugar-cane, while no one is there to receive the
money. Even a child would not think of helping
himself without paying the money. I am afraid that
an apple-woman's stall would not be as safe with
us. It would be thought thoroughly mean to steal
from any person so poor as to have to eke out his
living by the little street stall. Yet to appropriate
to one's own use the property of a rich man would
be thought no more robbery than many here would
think it robbery when robbing the government in
a matter of taxes or paying duty at the custom
house. A Chinese shopkeeper would probably see
no harm in overcharging a rich man who is able to
stand it, that he might sell at a reduced rate to a
poor man who needed the article for food. The
provision of the Mosaic law with regard to gleaning
is practiced by the Chinese in some of their crops.
Indeed, the humane spirit of the law of Moses is
exemplified in their standard of what is right. It
would be well if we Westerners, instead of always
standing up for our "rights," would allow the needs
of our fellow-men to weigh more in our decision.
Much of the strife between labor and capital, em-
ployer and employee might be avoided, and I am
persuaded we would be more virtuous in the sight
of God.

The Chinese in general are quiet and law-abiding,

though often excitable, and, in many places, turbulent and easily led into mob violence by those whom they look on as their natural leaders. Though wily enough to conceal their hands, the gentry are really at the bottom of most of the mobs in China. Of course China has her " dangerous classes," as other lands have. Yet China by no means has a monopoly of vice. In New York City where men of so many nationalities are gathered together, in 1893, 6 per cent. of the arrests were Chinese, while 9 per cent. were Irish, and the Italians and Russians each had 7 per cent. The Americans had 4 per cent., and the Germans 3 per cent. Considering race prejudice, and the fact that none of the policemen were Chinese, this is a fair showing.

Like all other nations, except possibly the most degraded tribes, the Chinese have natural consciences to which their classics frequently appeal. The decisions of these consciences coincide with the second table of the law ; though, as might be expected, being without a Divine revelation, the Chinese fail to discern the deeper meaning of these prohibitions as explained by our Saviour in the Sermon on the Mount. They have not taken in the fact that God's "commandment is exceeding broad," and applies equally to the "thoughts and intents of the heart " as to the external life.

But the Chinese frequently have dislocated consciences.   Like a joint out of place they inflict pain
where they ought not.   As the Pharisees constructed
a cumbrous system of minute observances and prohibitions, which were but a hideous excrescence
on the law of Moses, so the Chinese have "become vain in their imaginations, and their foolish
heart is darkened" under the influence of Buddhism and their childish reasonings.   I asked a
Chinaman once if he felt he was a sinner.   "Certainly," he replied.   "I have sometimes eaten beef,
and I have passed by written paper and let it be
trodden under foot instead of reverently picking it
up."

According to Chinese ethics it is wrong to eat
beef because the ox is used for plowing ; according to the morality of the Confucianists it is wrong
to permit a piece of paper with Chinese characters
written on it to be trodden under foot or used for
wrapping-paper, because it shows disrespect to the
sages.   It should all be "reverently collected" and
burnt.   The Chinese form benevolent societies who
employ men to go about the streets and pick up
every scrap of paper with characters printed or
written on it.   Boxes are placed along the streets
at convenient distances for the reception of such
paper, just as we put up our postal boxes.   On
these is the inscription, "Reverently spare written

TEMPLE OF FIVE HUNDRED GENII.—INTERIOR.

paper." I once asked a swearing, gambling man if
he were a filial son. He said, " How can I be? I
am too poor to buy a piece of pork as a present to
my father on his birthday." We think these things
amusing, but they are really part and parcel of the
every-day conscience of the ordinary Chinaman. As
the Pharisee neglected " the weightier matters of
the law " to pay tithes of " mint and anise and cum-
min," so many of the Chinese neglect the " truth and
righteousness" that their sages inculcate for these
senseless " traditions of the elders." Under the
blighting influence of misleading maxims and arti-
ficial requirements their conscience has become
blinded and misplaced. They sadly need the
authoritative word of God to set them right.

If I have not alluded to idolatry as a proof of
their perverted conscience, it is because it is too
plain to any intelligent reader to need mentioning.
As stated above, Chinese moralists seem to concentrate their attention on the second table of the law.
They do not emphasize man's duty to his Maker, for
they have no clear ideas concerning this Maker.
Their feeling seems to be : " Do right in the present,
and the future, if there be any future, will take care
of itself. Do your duty to your fellow-man, and you
have the best chance of gaining the favor of God,
if there be any God." They thus lose the strongest
sanction to morality. Paul, in summing up the sin-

fulness of man (Rom. iii.), says: "There is no fear of God before their eyes." When Confucius was asked about death, he said, "We do not yet know about life; how can we know about death?" This sentiment has impressed itself on the minds of his followers. God and a future world seem to be but visionary concerns, of secondary importance to the mind of the practical, earthly-minded Chinese. "The powers of the world to come" exert but little attraction on them. It is as if our earth knew only that force of gravitation which draws objects towards its center, and felt not that centripetal attraction which binds it to the sun. The approbation of future generations is the only immortality the Confucianist seeks for. This takes the place with him that the desire to please God and "enjoy Him forever," occupies in the mind of the Christian. While Christian morality has all the sanctions that Chinese morality has, it has the additional motive of a belief in God and in a future world. Kant says "Without a God, and without a world invisible to us now, but hoped for, the glorious ideas of ethics may indeed be objects of approbation and admiration, but cannot be the springs of purpose and action." Chinese Buddhism, it is true, has imagined a system of rewards and punishments in the future world, and representations of the ten Buddhist hells grace, or rather disgrace, the Government

municipal temples. But the Confucianists confess
that they have no faith in these silly inventions, but
use them merely to increase the deterrent effect of
the law among the ignorant masses by adding to its
penalties the fear of suffering in the future world.
Though these inventions of the priesthood are re-
jected by the more intelligent, they are not altogether without effect on the minds of the ignorant.
We must not be surprised, therefore, to see some
forms of vice and degradation more prevalent in
China than in Christendom.

Let us notice in detail some of the dangerous
tendencies which threaten the ruin of China as a
state.

OPIUM SMOKING.

The devil never made a wiser move than when he
introduced opium-smoking among the Chinese. It
just suits the natural disposition of the people, as
alcohol suits the active, impetuous disposition of the
West, and affords that stimulus which men fancy
they need to brace them against the cold, or prime
them up for trying exertion, so opium gives that
gentle excitement, and soporific effect which are en-
joyed by ease-loving Asiatics who are obliged, by
their poverty to labor hard, with poorly nourished
bodies, or who have no compunctions of conscience
as to self-indulgence or waste of time. The evil

effects of the habitual use of either of these stimulants are so obvious that it is unnecessary to draw any comparison between them. Perhaps an old medical missionary was not far out of the way when he said, " If a man must· choose between the two, let him smoke opium and go to the devil." If one drug is more violent in its effects, the other is more insidious ; if one leads a man to beat his family, the other may lead him to sell his wife and daughters as slaves. Opium is eating out the vitality of the Chinese people like a gangrene. It spares neither high nor low, men or women. Not that all indulge in it, or even a large proportion of the inhabitants of China, but it affects all classes. While those especially addicted to its use are the mandarins, students and under-officers connected with the Chinese Government offices, it is also largely used by the merchant class and by the lowest, most hardly worked coolies. While in many places it throws its fascinating bonds over but few of the women, in others, especially in Western China where it is largely raised, numbers of women and even of children are said to indulge in the enslaving habit.* It steals away the vigor of

* A gentleman well acquainted with Yunnan says : "Opium-smoking is general. Quite 80 per cent. of the men and 50 per cent. of the women take this pernicious drug, which undermines the constitution and ruins the health. It shortens the life of the consumer, and effects the population by producing sterility ; it paralyzes the moral nature, and prostrates the will : it is a fearful consumer of time, turning day

the police and soldiery, many of whom are habitual smokers. Probably one reason of the superior efficiency of the Japanese soldiers is that the use of opium is strictly forbidden in Japan. Its troops are physically inferior to those of China, (four feet eleven and a half inches being the standard of the Japanese army,) but their fighting qualities are far superior.

Wherever the Chinese go, they take their opium-smoking habit with them. In Siam, Cochin China, Singapore and other places on the peninsula of Malacca, and in Burma, a larger proportion are opium-smokers probably than in China itself; while in America and Australia many indulge in the deleterious habit, and open opium-joints to lead others to use the drug.

While opium was known in China before it was imported from India by foreigners, the habit of opium-smoking was not common. Upon the British East India Company must lie the blame of promoting the cultivation of the poppy in India and encouraging the use of the drug in China. Smuggled in at first, almost forced upon the Chinese as a result of the war of 1842—the so-called "Opium-war"—and legalized as a legitimate article of com-

into night, and night into day. It is rapidly effecting a very general deterioration, and threatens to transmute an industrious people into anationof helpless idlers and imbeciles."

merce by the treaty following the Anglo-French war of 1856, its use soon spread fearfully in the maritime provinces. The cultivation of the native article was also rapidly increased in order to supply the increasing demand for the poison. Over $30,-000,000 are now annually spent for the imported drug alone. Not only in Yunnan and Sze Chuen provinces is the poppy extensively grown, but in many others parts of the empire. The Chinese Government has always regarded the use of opium as harmful and a source of decay to the state. The Emperor Tao Kwang, when urged to legalize the traffic and tax the drug, uttered that noble sentiment, "I can never consent to derive an income from the vices of my subjects!" But the corruption of Chinese officialdom is so great that the drug was introduced by the connivance of the Government officers as well as by force.

Opium becomes a source of danger to the state and an element in natural decay by absorbing the land which would otherwise be used for producing food. The wheat and corn and barley converted into beer and whisky, according to the testimony of many physicians, do not entirely lose their food-value. Then, too, in times of famine or scarcity of food, the cereals would be used directly as food instead of being converted into alcohol. But with opium it is different; it has no value as a food, is so much easier of transportation, and always brings so much better price, that even the sternest repressive measures will fail to prevent its cultivation. The area of the cultivation of cereals being diminished renders the land more liable to be afflicted by famine.

Another reason why opium tends to destroy the stability of the state, is that it eats out the virility and undermines the energies of the individual. While, as is the case with whisky, a few seem to be able to take large quantities with impunity, with the vast majority this is not the case. Men lose their healthy color and their flesh, become peevish, restless and discontented until their accustomed dose soothes them into apathy and somnolence. The reproductive functions are diminished and the children are apt to be puny and deficient in vigor. An old merchant who had done business with the Chinese for some fifty years, told me that he had seen the families of some of the wealthiest and most influential Chinese merchants grow impaired in body and mind, dwindle down and become extinct from indulgence in the fascinating drug. Victims of the poison grow old before their time, and lose their appetite for nutritious food. They are apt to speak with the piping tones, and move with the jerky motions of senility and imbecility. It must sap the strength of a state to have its leaders and its soldiers sink into such a condition.

As to its effects on the family of the sot, there is not much to choose between opium and whisky. It is true, opium does not often excite the Chinese to deeds of violence and lead a man to beat his wife and children. But the craving caused by the use of either drug is the same. In order to get money to satisfy his depraved appetite a man will steal and pawn his wife's clothes, his furniture, the garments off his children's back or anything he can lay his hands on. He loses all sense of self-respect, and nothing is too mean or degrading for him. He will sell his daughter into bondage, and sometimes even sell his wife to another man. His diseased appetite holds him fast in its iron chains. Thus opium-smoking is a foul ulcer upon the body politic, spreading its poison through all ranks of society and threatening the vitality of the state.

MOHOMEDAN MOSQUE WITH WATCH-TOWER.

CHAPTER VII.

DESTRUCTIVE FORCES—CONTINUED.

GAMBLING.

LIKE the craving for stimulants, love of gambling is not restricted to any nation or people. The European has his cards and roulette tables, the Malay his cock-fighting, the Chinaman his cards, dominoes and *fan-tan*, while almost all lands have their dice, their lotteries and their betting. Perhaps the fairest and simplest form, where all opportunity for cheating would seem to be excluded, is that used by the Persians, where each man takes out his lump of sugar, makes his wager, and the one whose lump attracts the first fly wins the prize. Like profane swearing, gambling may be a perversion of what may at first have been an act of worship—an appeal to Deity to settle a matter. "The lot is cast into the lap, but the whole disposing thereof is of the Lord," says Solomon. Lots have been cast before idol deities from time immemorial and in all heathen lands. A certain form of divination is highly praised and was reverently believed in by Confucius,

and is regarded as sacred by the Chinese to the
present day.   Oracles and various methods of con-
sulting the gods by lot are in common use in every
Chinese temple.   But the element of chance may
be the only link which connects these religious
observances with the ordinary gambling for gain
which is so prevalent in China.   The Chinese learn
to gamble from their very childhood.   The little
stalls on the street and by the roadside where fruit
and nuts and sweetmeats are sold to the children, frequently have their dice, wheels-of-fortune, etc., where
a child, by staking one cash, may have the chance of
winning the worth of two.   On feast days and holi-
days, gambling games of all kinds abound, and
children are enticed to venture their spending money
in traps of all kinds.

Gambling is begotten of and begets that idleness
which is so common in China.   Though the Chinese
are an industrious race, yet they have a great deal
of spare time.   They spend much of their time sit-
ting together smoking and conversing.   It is not
strange that they seek for some excitement to break
the monotony of their humdrum lives.   If you go
into a village you find the young men gathered together after their day of hard toil.   What are they
to do ?   They have no newspapers, and if they had,
are to ignorant to enjoy reading them, they are
without books, except perhaps their old school-

books; if there be a gaming table there, what so
natural as that they should gather around it to
watch the game and stake their spare cash?
The fondness for gaming once acquired, especially
if they have succeeded in winning some money,
they are only too glad to exchange the dull monotony of hard toil in the rice fields for the excitement
and indolence of the gaming table. Especially
on market-days is gambling found in full blast.
Numerous gambling booths are found in almost
all the market towns. Here are assembled the
sharpers, the indolent, the worthless and the desperate. No mercy is shown to the poor wretch
who loses; his clothes are stripped off his back and
he is sent off with cuffs and curses if he does not
at once pay what he loses. So in the purlieus of
the cities, numerous colonies of gamblers are found.
Tables for *fan-tan* and mats spread on the ground
with dice are in open sight to entrap the unwary,
like spiders' webs to catch the thoughtless, listless
fly. In the business parts of the city rooms are
rented for gambling, while the pimps stand at the
door to invite the simple with their stereotyped invitation: " Buy a chance and get rich." Besides
these back rooms with their gaming tables for the
common people, more expensive establishments are
gotten up for the rich where only gold or silver are
accepted in wagers. Though most of the gamblers

are men, gambling is not confined to them. Some
of the women, especially those who are well off and
have leisure, pass away the time which hangs so
heavily on their hands by gambling at cards or
dominoes, and in the excitement of the game frequently stake their gold and silver hair-pins and
bangles and other pieces of jewelry.

This passion for gambling seems to be innate
with the Chinese. They often defend it as being
perfectly fair, and seem to have no moral objections
to the principle as long as only small sums are
wagered. But Chinese statesmen see in it rightly
a menace to society. It gathers the dissolute, the
shiftless, the rascal and the idler together. Em-
ployees are tempted to stake their employers'
money in the hope of gaining something for themselves; men neglect their business and lose their
employers' time; the public peace is broken by
fights and bloodshed among the desperate characters who keep and frequent the gaming tables, and
the nests of gamblers become hot-beds for all kinds
of crime. The law therefore forbids gambling, and
the officers occasionally make a raid on the gambling
houses. But the gamblers are usually men who
have been in government employ, and generally are
under the protection of some one in authority.
Hush money is paid and spies are always on the
alert, so that they are not often caught.

Beside card-playing and gaming tables, lotteries are a form of gambling much patronized by the Chinese. These are not open to the objection of assembling bad characters where they can concoct robberies and other evil schemes. Hence they are dealt with more leniently. Though illegal, they are sometimes farmed out by the officials when hard pressed for money. Immense sums are lost annually in these lotteries. There are several forms of lotteries, among which the most common are the *peh-koh-piau* or "white-dove tickets," or guessing a number of characters in a list, instead of numbers as in our lotteries; and the *wei-sing*, or wagering on the successful candidate in a government examination, as we bet on elections or on a horse-race. The Chinese method seems to be fairer than ours, as there is less opportunity of influencing the result, for the bet is not on an individual but that a certain *surname* will succeed.

Gambling, as it promotes a spirit of unrest and of idleness, as it leads men to seek to win money rather than earn it, as it leads men to squander their means and reduce their families to poverty, is always a source of danger to the state. The Chinese government seems to be aware of this fact even more keenly than the Western ones are, but seems unable to help itself, and impotent to exert any real control over the gambling habit which seems to be so innate in the people and to have its ramifications throughout the Empire.   With that desire for some excitement to break the monotony of their lives, that greed of gain and disposition to slide into indolence, and that laxity of moral principle, which are so marked in the Chinese character, it is to be feared that this source of decadence will increase rather than decrease under present conditions.

CRUELTY.

The Chinese have always had the name of being a cruel people.   Perhaps nothing more than this fact has led Western nations to feel that they have not far emerged from barbarism.   The classics tell that some of the ancient kings were monsters of cruelty, and how they seemed to take delight in inflicting needless and excruciating pain on their helpless victims.   In this respect China seems never to have gotten beyond the stage of barbarism. Human life is held very cheap, and may be sacrificed with impunity at the caprice of the sovereign.

Cruelty to animals is thought nothing of.   The Chinese in this respect seem not to have passed out of the boyhood stage.   The sufferings of the inferior animals seem to excite laughter rather than pity.   It is no wonder that they are esteemed a hard-hearted race. I have seen a rat nailed by its four outstretched paws to a board and left for hours or days until it died. I have seen a dog tortured to death in a most cruel way. The tendency of Buddhism seems to lead to kindness to animals, and yet, among the Chinese, while it has led some to think it to be wrong to take animal life, it does not seem to have led them to see any harm in inflicting suffering on helpless animals.

Cramping the feet of their little girls is another instance of the light regard which they have for needless suffering. That their hearts are not touched by the intense pain of their own offspring, endured through days, weeks and months, shows how insensible they have become. The Manchu government is not responsible for this cruel practice as the Manchus do not practice it themselves, and they have often tried to suppress it among the Chinese, but in vain. As the Chinese say, "Fashion is stronger than the Emperor."

The destroying of female infants is another cruel practice that the Manchus have tried to put down, but cannot prevent. Chinese moralists, too, have decried the custom, but without success. A missionary lady asked a crowd of women around her how many of them had drowned their infants, and all confessed to have killed one at least, and one acknowledged that she had destroyed five. In some

parts of China this is much more common than in
others. Poverty and inability to raise so many
children is the excuse they give for their cruelty.
Thus cruelty tends to depopulate the country. Pre-
natal infanticide is also very common. They sometimes prefer drowning the infant to abortion, as they
do not wish to destroy the boys.

But the worst manifestation of Chinese cruelty
is seen in their treatment of their prisoners, whether
those taken in war or imprisoned in the ordinary
jails. This is not surprising when we consider how
recently similar cruelties were practiced by so-called
Christian nations. In this respect, China is a piece
of ancient Assyria or Babylonia, placed in the midst
of the nineteenth century. It is to be feared that
the Chinese respect for the past makes them indif-
ferent to the sufferings of their fellow-men, especially those who are accused or convicted of crime.
It is true the refined and excessive cruelty of some
of the ancient rulers is condemned in the classics,
still the ordinary punishments of ancient times would
be thought outrageous under our Christian civilization. The legal punishments under the present
dynasty are nothing like so severe as the extra legal
torture inflicted in the courts, and at least winked
at, if not encouraged, by those in authority. The
Chinese are a stubborn and untruthful race, and
their officers no doubt find great difficulty in extort-

LITERARY PAGODA.

ing the truth in any case which comes before them. The verbal testimony of a witness is nearly worthless, as he is easily bribed and will ordinarily never tell the truth if he has the least chance to tell a falsehood. It is not surprising that the mandarins are often provoked, and have learned by experience to put no confidence in the testimony of witnesses. As with us a criminal will usually plead " not guilty," however conscious he may be that he has committed the offense, so, among the Chinese, the accused will stoutly deny that he is guilty of the crime charged. The great object of the judge is to get him to confess. The Chinese proverb is, " If you are charged with stealing a well, you must confess." The magistrate must either entangle him in his talk so as to get the equivalent of a confession, or he must extort the confession through bodily suffering. When annoyed at the pertinacity or boldness of the prisoner, the judge may order all kinds of cruel tortures in order to force the man to acknowledge his guilt. Giving men hundreds of strokes, beating them until the flesh is lacerated, putting on thumbscrews, or making them kneel on chains while the torturers jump on each end of a bamboo placed in the bend of the knee, and other horrid cruelties are frequently practiced on a helpless prisoner. It is not strange that a foreigner, seeing the cruelties of a Chinese court, exclaimed : " Thank God, there is a hell where these wretches who, clothed with brief authority, inflict such pain on their helpless fellow-men, will receive the due reward for their cruelty." A Chinaman who was educated in Europe and spoke English and French with facility, practiced such horrible cruelties on political prisoners that the foreign consuls at the port refused to pay or receive visits from him or have any official relations with him.

Prisoners are subjected to untold privations and suffering by their keepers, in order to extort money from them, or compel their friends to pay the keepers to remit their cruelties. Any one who has visited the dark, dirty dungeons of a Chinese prison will feel that even the tender mercies of the wicked are cruel. The horrors of an Eastern prison excite the utmost disgust and indignation in the minds of those who are acquainted with the clean and orderly appearance of Western jails, and penitentiaries. Several years ago a Chinese literary man who was caught in the meshes of the law and obliged to spend some time in a jail in Canton, wrote a pamphlet in which he described in vivid colors the horrors and cruelties practiced by the jailers.

Crucifixion is an extra-legal punishment not unfrequently inflicted on noted pirates and robbers. The legal punishments are comparatively mild, if we except the *ling chi*, " the slow and lingering " punishment inflicted on parricides, women who kill their husbands, and occasionally on political criminals. This consists in cutting slices off of the breasts, arms and thighs, before the prisoner is put to death.

In the treatment of their prisoners captured in war, the Chinese seem to delight in cruelty. It was the beheading and mutilating of the Japanese prisoners at Port Arthur, that excited these men to commit the massacre at that stronghold. I was once traveling with a Chinese officer, who was describing the capture of a rebel officer at Nankin. He seemed to gloat over the sufferings he inflicted on his unfortunate prisoner. He told how he strung him up and shot and stabbed him, and said, "If you want to die, I won't let you die ; if you want to live, I won't let you live." This, I am persuaded, is no exception to the sentiments the Chinese soldiers usually cherish towards their enemies who are so unfortunate as to fall into their hands.

The inhumanity of the Chinese is seen in the treatment of their own wounded in battle. A gentleman writing recently from Tien-tsin, says : "The Chinese indifference to their wounded has been to me the worst feature in this war." The *Taotai*, the highest official in that city, when appealed to by foreigners who felt for the sufferings of the Chinese soldiers, said heartlessly: "What do I want with wounded men ? The sooner they die the

better. China has plenty of men." This heathenish callousness to the sufferings of one's own men
seems strange to us, but it does not strike the
Chinese so.

Several years ago Marquis Tseing, the Chinese
ambassador to England, wrote an article for an
English review entitled, "China's Awakening," in
which he stated that the great need of China was
modern ships and armaments. A Chinese lawyer in
Hong Kong, who had been educated in England,
replied that China's first and greatest need was reform in her legal procedure and prison discipline.
The cruelties practiced by the Chinese show that
China is out of touch with Western nations and still on
the confines of barbarism. Though men may try to
find many excuses for such conduct; it is undoubtedly
a source of weakness in a state, as it alienates the
feelings of the people from their rulers, and makes
men unwilling to risk their lives in military service.
Then it makes, and justly too, more enlightened
nations look down on the Chinese as still akin to
barbarians, and treat them accordingly. When
Japan took on herself Western civilization, prison
reform held a prominent place in her advancement,
and the Côde Napoleon was adopted as the basis of
her legal procedure. By her improved code she
has advanced in the affection of her own subjects,
as well as in the respect of foreign nations.

UNTRUTHFULNESS.

The Chinese sages are loud in their praises of Truth and Righteousness, but the Chinese people are noted for their practical rejection of both of these virtues. Truthfulness cannot be called an Asiatic virtue. A Chinaman once remarked to me: "Men are all alike; all want to accomplish their own ends. The only difference between Chinese and Westerners is, you seek to accomplish your ends by boldness and force, and we try to accomplish ours by cunning and duplicity." This remark shows the difference between Asiatic and European ideas in a nutshell. To illustrate his point he said: "You foreigners come here with your war vessels and extort a treaty from us; of course we try to evade it every way we can when the force is withdrawn. It is perfectly fair—cunning against force."

In this matter the whole nation is rotten from top to bottom. Mutual confidence is about dead. Their system of governing does not encourage truthfulness. The courts of the officials to whom the people are taught to look up to as patterns, are fountains of lying and injustice. Even the highest officials seem utterly without any sense of honor, as we understand the word. Men are not only careless with regard to keeping their word, but even an oath has

7

little or no binding effect. A consul told me that a Chinese viceroy, then and now high in the counsels of the nation, had requested to be allowed to examine the deeds to a piece of land, which were on file at the consulate, and when the favor had been granted him, on the supposition that one so high in authority would certainly keep his word, not only refused to return the deed, but utterly ignored frequent dispatches requesting him to do so. No doubt he chuckled over the thought that he had played a sharp trick on the foreign barbarian.

The Chinese trust nothing to the honor of the students who attend the Government examinations. Though they are grown men, their persons are searched as they enter the enclosure to see if they are carrying any books or helps of any kind with them; searched as even our schoolboys would not submit to, and as a policeman would search a man under arrest. Nor is this without a cause, as most of the students would descend to the most cunning tricks to deceive the examiners. "Sleeve editions" of the classics are published in the finest type and most portable shape, so that they may be concealed in the sleeves of the candidates. Copies are hidden in the soles of their shoes, the lining of their clothes and among their food. The Government goes on the supposition that every man is a cheat, because they have learned by long experience that that is a fact with regard to the great majority of those with whom they have to deal. Even high officials are not trusted, but are under the surveillance of censors and secret emissaries from Peking. Where lying and dishonesty are so rife, of course bribery is a common thing.

Many offices are obtained through bribery in some form or other. When you see an honest official, and there are some of this kind in China, he is like a man walking on ice, and he finds it very difficult to keep his foothold against those who are trying to trip him up or push him down.

The Chinese seem to lie and prevaricate naturally, and to tell the truth is like losing a tooth. You can rarely trust in what a man says when it would be his *interest* to utter a falsehood. So, in dealing with a man, you always have to consider first where his interest lies, before you can determine how much weight to attach to his words. When they assign a reason for an act they are apt to emphasize some minor reason which may possibly have some slight bearing on the case, while they studiously conceal the main, true reason. Perhaps the tendency of the human mind to say what is not so is nowhere seen more clearly than in conventionalities of polite society. This is eminently true in China. The Chinese have a great deal of true politeness and consideration for the feelings of others. But they often carry it too far, and have no hesitation in sacrificing the truth to appear to be polite. Many of the ordinary forms of politeness and hospitality are mere shams; as when the Chinaman complained of the incivility of a visitor, saying, " I was polite enough to ask him to dinner, and he was not polite enough to decline the invitation." You are always invited to remain for a meal, but no one is expected to accept the invitation, unless he really is a friend from abroad. I do not mean to say that this form of untruthfulness is peculiar to China, but only that it abounds there.

In buying and selling, very few Chinese shop-keepers have a fixed price for their goods. As you go into a shop you see the wily salesman " taking your measure " to see how much he will charge you. If he thinks you are ignorant of the true value of what you ask for, or are in great need of it, or have little time to spend in your purchase, he will charge you about double the value and enjoy the contest of wits as you try to beat him down. He rarely gets excited but smugly smiles, especially if the purchaser shows any annoyance at the hag-gling. The lack of downright integrity and truth-fulness is everywhere apparent.

No argument is needed to prove that untruthful-ness is an element of decay in a state. Distrust saps the foundations of things. There can be no

JUNKS AND BOATS.

patriotism where the people have no confidence in the promises and honor of the government. The bonds which unite society are loosened when men are filled with suspicion and distrust of one another. Sectional jealousies and mutual suspicions have much to do with the want of unity in the counsels of China.

If I have not dwelt upon the influence of false systems of religion in misleading the mind in the highest sphere of its activity, it is because I have considered truthfulness as a social virtue rather than from a religious point of view. Still, the connection between the two things is by no means a slight one, and history will show that in lands where the revealed word of the God of truth is known and He who is " the Truth " is reverenced, all truth is honored and all untruthfulness is looked upon as a disgrace. When we remember that " whosoever loveth and maketh a lie " is under the curse of God, we can understand why China cannot expect His blessing until untruthfulness shall cease to be so characteristic of her people.

CHAPTER VIII.

DESTRUCTIVE FORCES—CONTINUED
INJUSTICE.

THE most common complaint of the Chinese, except, perhaps, the ever-present cry of " hard times," so common in every land, is the injustice of the courts. They have no confidence either in the integrity of their mandarins or the possibility of obtaining justice at their hands. It is difficult to see how they can have such confidence when they know that almost every office is bought, and that even when an officer desires to do right, all access to him is blocked by a number of underlings who have to be bribed before they will admit any one into his presence. While in criminal cases no doubt substantial justice is done when a man is really guilty, in civil suits there is no certainty whatever. Whoever has the longest purse or the heaviest " pull," stands the best chance of gaining his cause. Even in criminal cases money has great influence. While almost any decision may be obtained through money, no decision can be secured without it. It is not always that the mandarin desires to do wrong, but the truth is withheld, and so many false statements are made that his judgment is warped by those through whom the case is brought before him. Though lawyers are forbidden to practice in the courts, there is a class of pettifoggers who make their living by drawing up all kinds of lying charges.

Where crime is committed the officers are not so particular about punishing the actual criminal. So *some one* suffers the penalty, that is sufficient. Suppose a man reports that his store has been attacked by a band of eight robbers, the police are ordered to arrest the robbers within a fixed time. If by the expiry of this time they do not bring at least four men, they themselves are beaten. They try to secure some of the real offenders, but if they fail to find them, or the men or their friends bribe them, they may lay hold on any common thief or worthless character of whom the community is glad to get rid, and take him to make up the number. There are sometimes hangers-on about the courts who are willing to personate the offender and take a beating in his stead if they are well paid for it. So the majesty of the law is vindicated by a penalty being inflicted, and so the magistrate escapes the reprimand of his superiors for letting the crime go unpunished, the case is considered as settled satisfactorily

The clan feeling is very strong in China, and men are looked upon rather as members of a community than as individuals. In feuds between two villages it is not so much the actual murderer who is demanded in reparation, as some one from the clan which he represents. They are satisfied with the same clumsy justice that we sometimes exercise in war in making reprisals, where not the real offender suffers the penalty, but any one belonging to the same side. Thus punishing the guiltless does not strike the Chinese as the enormity it presents to our eyes. Any one who associates with or belongs to the criminal class may be made to suffer the penalty actually due some other member of that class, and it will be looked on by the community as a good riddance. I mention these things only to show how, according to our ideas, the Chinese notions of justice are obscured. It is not these occasional failures, but the gross miscarriages of justice in their courts that give rise to the complaints against the mandarins.

It is not necessary to dwell longer on this point. Any one can readily see how injustice on the part of those in authority weakens the attachment of the people to their government.

POLYGAMY.

Under this head I shall include all those practices which tend to debase woman below her proper

sphere. There can be no real improvement in a
state unless both sexes are progressing, and advance
side by side. If the mother is degraded, the son is
pulled down with her. If the mother is ignorant,
superstitious, bad-tempered, trifling, unchaste, the
sons as well as the daughters will suffer.

As a general thing the Chinese women are industrious, modest and chaste. Nothing can exceed
the modesty of their dress and their behavior on the
street. Of course there are abandoned women who
give themselves up to all manner of lewdness. But
even many of these are to be pitied more than
blamed, for they are generally sold or stolen while
little girls and brought up for the life they lead,
and have not entered upon it of their own will.
Those who do not belong to the class of prostitutes,
are usually, except perhaps some servants, chaste.
There is no such unbridled exhibitions of indecency
and lust in society as at the French ball in New
York, or in the ballet in some theaters. In this regard the East can put the West to the blush.

A heathen social economist, looking at things
from a purely physical point of view, might defend
polygamy as tending to keep up the bodily vigor of
the race, for the concubines of a wealthy man are
almost always taken from the stronger working class
of women, while the chief wife is a small-footed
woman of delicate build, from the same class as the

husband himself. The offspring of the former
would probably prove more vigorous and healthy.
There may be some truth in this, but any advantage in this direction is more than counterbalanced
by the moral degeneration which ensues from a child
being brought up in the atmosphere of a family
where bickerings and quarrels, intrigues and jealousies are of almost daily occurrence. There is
nothing answering to a home according to our ideas
of the word. The Chinese proverb says : " One
key doesn't rattle," by which they mean if there is
but one wife there will be peace, but if there are
more, there is sure to be strife. The lives of Sarah
and Hagar, of Leah and Rachel, give a true picture of an Eastern household with polygamy. This
practice tends to degrade woman and make her a
toy or a slave instead of a true companion.

While in most parts of China woman has more
freedom and meets with more consideration than in
Mohammedan countries and in India, still she is
looked down upon and considered an inferior. She
has few or no rights. Her education is neglected,
and it is a very rare thing to find a woman who
can read or write. While many of them have good
minds, susceptible of taking even an advanced training, their education is neglected, and to cook, wash
and sew is looked upon as the sum of female duties.
As the girls are looked upon as going out of the

family and belonging to another when they are married, and they are married early, it is thought a waste of time and of money to spend them on their education. Growing up without mental training, subject to much drudgery and abuse, they grow up with little ambition or hope. It is only as a mother, and especially as the mother of a son, that a Chinese woman seems to have any enjoyment in life. The mother-love is the one sunbeam that brightens their lives. For ages looked down upon as little better than a slave, woman has learned to accommodate herself to what is expected of her, and too often her character fails to rise to what it might be under better influences. In the Chinese language all that is weak, mean, little and debased is written with the radical for *woman* in it. Thus their estimate of the sex has become a part of the very language itself.

I have already alluded to foot-binding and to the destruction of female infants. These practices, so common in China, are only additional facts to show the estimation of the sex among the Chinese. Their cruel treatment of blind girls is another thing which shows how far below the Christian standard of civilization and enlightenment the Chinese people are. The parents of these unfortunate girls find themselves with their daughters on their hands without any prospect either of marrying or of contributing to the support of the family by their industry. So, too often they sell them to vile hags who train them to play the lute and send them out on the streets at night to earn their living as singing girls. They sing lewd songs and have to submit to all kinds of familiarity and indignity that they may earn a pittance for their mistresses. They are treated with great cruelty and are beaten if they do not return with something earned during the night. It is a common sight in Canton to see strings of six or eight of these girls, led by an old woman, going about the streets to ply their vocation. Their sunken eyes and sad, thin faces, together with the thought of the miserable lives they are forced to lead, are enough to excite the pity of the most unemotional. The Chinese speak of the houses where these poor girls are trained as, " little hells," so notorious are the cruelties practiced upon the inmates. Though the Government has a blind asylum where a little aid is given to the blind, it has remained for Christian philanthropy to feel an interest in the blind girls and try to save them.

This neglect and unfair treatment of women must prove an element of weakness in the state. The whole population must be uplifted ; if the half be ignored, Society cannot rise to the plane it should occupy in a truly enlightened state.

EXAMINATION HALL.—EXAMINERS' OFFICES.

THE DANGEROUS CLASSES.

Of course what are termed the " dangerous classes," are a threat to the stability of any government. They are made up of the unemployed, the idle, the vicious, the discontented, and those who, though they eat, contribute nothing to the production of the country. All lands have their share of these men, whether called anarchists, socialists, rowdies, or the proletariat. China, with singular fatuity and short-sightedness, adds to the number of these men in her midst, forgetful of the fact that she is increasing the probabilities of her own downfall. The regular army in China is used mainly to garrison the walled cities, while the actual fighting is carried on by means of volunteers or " braves," who are recruited from among the young men. At the end of a campaign these men are turned loose, with no pensions, often with their pay in arrears and they themselves away from their homes. It is not strange that many of them turn pirates, robbers and gamblers. The habits of license formed in the camp, and of roving about the country under the loosest kind of discipline, remain with them after they are discharged. One reason why piracy and highway robbery are so hard to put down is that the pirates and robbers are old acquaintances and comrades of the very men who are sent against them. The law-

8

less habits of the Chinese soldiery are well known. In all wars foraging is bad enough, but in China the commissariat arrangements are so imperfect that the soldiers frequently live off of the country folk by helping themselves to what they want. In the Tai Peng rebellion it was said that the people often dreaded the Imperial troops more than they did the rebels, and recently it is stated that in Moukden the populace feared the coming of their own troops much more than that of the Japanese. These free-booting habits tend to make a lot of discharged soldiers a plague to the country where they are mustered out of service. The gaming tables, forbidden by law, but winked at by the authorities, help to perpetuate this class of shiftless, idle men who have nothing to lose and are ever ready for any popular tumult or anything to turn up. Were it not for the almost constant risings and rebellions that occur in various parts of the Empire where these men find employment either as rebels or as soldiers, the plague would probably be worse than it is, for these dangerous men are thus gathered together instead of being scattered all about the land.

It may well be seen how the large number of these discontented, desperate men, constantly recruited from the gaming table and the camp, are a menace to the prosperity and stability of the Government and a source of decay in the state.

I have thus tried to glance at some of the destructive tendencies which exist in China. To the thoughtful Chinese statesman they must appear a baleful menace to the existing state, and should claim his serious attention as evils which are surely, even though but slowly it may be, undermining the stability of the Empire. They should lead him to ask whether some reform is not demanded, whether some change is not needed. They should make him inquire whether that Conservatism under which they have grown up is, after all, the best thing for China, and whether some advancement in the line of a Christian civilization may not be possible.

CHAPTER IX.

RECONSTRUCTIVE FORCES.

But let us turn from the somber picture of the past and look towards the future. I am persuaded there is hope for China. There are Reconstructive Forces at work as well as Destructive ones; the leaven of Progress has been introduced which will eventually leaven the dull lump of Conservatism. As yet China has moved only in response to efforts from without, but her true regeneration will result only from a force from within. The seed is influenced by its environment, the warmth and the moisture, but the growth and full development of the plant depends on the starting of the germ within. I am persuaded that the Chinese have within them the elements of a stalwart, reliable character. While in many regards Asiatics, they, like the Jews, have many characteristics which remind us of Occidentals. They have the industry, the enterprise, the perseverance, the practical common sense which mark the Anglo-Saxons. They are born merchants and have all the elements of success in business. They have the instinct for organization, and scarcely ever, even in their smallest communities, exist in an amorphous mass, but easily crystallize into guilds and societies. Their theoretical moral standards are not low, though, under the influence of gross materialism and earthliness, their practical maxims are much degraded. Under the stress and strain of the struggle for existence they are too apt to cast aside their ideas of what they know to be right; still they admit the force of these ideas.

China is a sleeping elephant which resents having its slumbers disturbed. She has abundant resources, but is slow to develop them. She has a reserve stock of energy, but does not know how properly to exert it. China is like a man overtaken by a snowstorm, who succumbs to the cold and wishes simply to go to sleep and be let alone. She resents the energy of the St. Bernard dogs which would arouse her and drag her into a place of safety. Conscious of her vast resources, she wonders why other nations do not fear arousing her anger. But the rough awakening will yet be her salvation. When she is once aroused and learns the truth that it is " righteousness that exalteth a nation," we may hope that her true regeneration will set in. For one I believe in the integrity and vitality of China. I hope she will never be disintegrated nor come under the rule of any foreign power. I trust she may learn to

put away her innate self-conceit that is hurrying
her to ruin, and that her eyes may be opened to
see her true position among the nations of the
world.   If she would only learn to substitute
honesty and square-dealing for duplicity and crafti-
ness her advancement would be greatly hastened.
Her present disastrous war with Japan would
probably have been averted but for her intriguing,
double-faced policy in Korea.

China's awakening must come from two sources:
first, from free intercourse with the rest of the
world, and, secondly, from Christianity permeating
every part of the Empire, and leavening and re-
molding its institutions.   These reconstructive forces
are already beginning to work; to them let us now
direct our attention.

We cannot close our eyes to the fact that the
pressure from without, which is changing the face
of affairs in China, has come from war.   Terrible
as it is, war has been the prelude and even the
immediate cause of most of the changes that have
taken place in history.   It is like the cyclone that
spreads devastation in its path, uprooting primeval
forests, prostrating the most costly constructions of
man, and destroying human life by its terrific force,
but purifying the atmosphere, and making life
possible by removing the germs of disease and
death.   A temporary evil results in permanent

blessing. As in Nature, so in History. God often accomplishes His beneficent purposes by violent means. Even unjust wars often result in beneficial consequences. The Psalmist speaks of the wicked as God's sword. Even wars undertaken through human greed and pride, and unhallowed ambition, may result in good. While they are no doubt often chastisements sent by God upon a nation, like other chastisements, they may bring forth the fruit of righteousness. It is through war that China has been opened. The war of 1842—the so-called " Opium war "—though morally unjustifiable, was one that might have occurred between any two nations ; high-handed destruction of property was followed by a demand for indemnity and hostilities. It proved the entering wedge for Western inter-course with China, and an effected entrance through the wall of seclusion, with which the Chinese had surrounded themselves. Much as we may regret it, the fact remains, that, when an opening is made, the good and the bad flow in together. The same ship which takes the messenger of the Gospel to Africa, carries a cargo of rum ; the same steamer that conveys the missionary to China, carries opium in her hold. As in the man, so in the nation. The boy passes out of the period of innocence into that of virtue (*virtus*) when his character is formed by his *choices* between good and evil ; it is only thus that the boy becomes the true man. So, in the Providence of God, it would seem that nations pass from the stage of " the state of nature " into a higher one, only by having the good and the evil presented together, that they may take their choice. To the philanthropist it seems sad that such should be the case, and yet it seems a necessity incident to that state of probation through which our race is passing, and a prelude to that separation into two classes which will be consummated at the day of judgment. However strongly we may oppose the curse of rum and of opium, and however earnestly we may regret the evils of war, as students of history we cannot ignore the facts we see around us.

As the result of war, then, China has been opened to *Commerce.* Though commerce brings its evils as well as its benefits, in the long run it is beneficial to the prosperity of a country. The standard of living is raised, comforts are multiplied and the mental horizon is widened. Trade has prospered in all the ports opened to foreigners, the interchange of commodities has been a source of revenue to the Government as well as of prosperity to the people. Production has increased, and men have made fortunes as middle-men as well as carriers. New ideas have been kindled in the sluggish minds of the people, and new articles have been introduced. Steamers owned by the natives are traversing the

BUDDHIST PAGODA.

rivers of China, giving employment to many through the increase of Trade. Machinery and new arts have been introduced to some extent, and the dog-trot pace of the people has been quickened to a faster step. Time has become of appreciable value. The mere fact that steamers leave on time has put a new life into the people. The sharp competitions of trade have put men on the alert. One has but to go through the streets of the Chinese portion of Hong Kong or Shanghai, and then through those of some inland town away from the quickening influence of foreign trade, to see the difference. While morally all business marts tend to become Corinths, and spirituality is apt to be swallowed up in the greedy quest for gain, the minds of men are quickened, and external prosperity at least is flourishing. The resources of China have been developed by foreign intercourse as they never would have been without it. China's trade in the open ports amounted, in 1891, to $950,000,000, and the increase during the decade, 1881–1891, amounted to 50 per cent. Were it not for the pressure brought to bear by foreign nations (especially by England), to whom 60 per cent. of the commerce is credited in the Customs reports, China would kill the goose that lays the golden egg, and stifle the efforts of her own merchants by all kinds of exactions, and restrictions forbidden by the treaties. The policy of seclusion has not yet been abandoned oy China. Though her principal ports have been opened to trade and have been prospered by trade, the country at large is still closed. All concessions to trade are yielded unwillingly, inch by inch. While some temporary evils might ensue from all China being thrown open to foreign intercourse, no doubt, commercially, it would be an advantage to the people. It is almost bound to come, sooner or later, for, with the present means of intercommunication between all parts of the world, it is impossible for one people to shut itself off from the rest of mankind. The demands of commerce are never satisfied, and commerce has been and probably will yet be one of the most powerful reconstructive agencies in China.

IMPERIAL MARITIME CUSTOMS.

The Foreign Customs Service, under the able administration of Sir Robert Hart, has been one of the main levers used to prize China out of the bog of conservatism in which she had sunk for so long, and it probably will be one of the main dependencies for her elevation in the future. Upon the close of the Anglo-French war of 1859, an arrangement was made by which the customs dues at the treaty ports were to be collected by a corps of foreigners. This service was placed first under Mr. Lay, and then under Sir Robert Hart, the present Inspector-General. Under his wise administration this has been the entering wedge for many important improvements in China. Efficient officers have been secured, an honest administration established, tradal relations extended, and the Imperial exchequer greatly augmented, so that now trade to the amount of nearly a billion of dollars is carried on annually in the open ports. Through the intelligent researches of thoroughly trained men, made known to the world in occasional and annual reports, the resources, productions, botany, arts, and diseases of the Chinese have been described as never before. The Chinese have been made acquainted with the Western methods of a progressive, honest and economical administration. A postal system has been organized, a system of light-houses and buoys has been established, navigation has been improved, and a general impetus has been given to advancement in the line of progress. The daily intercourse between Chinese officials and clerks with able, educated men from the West must have taught them to look with respect upon the acquirements and culture which result from a Christian civilization. However self-conceited they may be, it is impossible for them to look down upon these representatives of the West as mere " outside barbarians." Nor has the influence of the Inspector-General and some of the

Commissioners been small in directing the policy of the nation. Being still under the protection of their native lands, they can speak to the higher authorities with a frankness and honesty which a Chinaman would not venture to use for fear of losing his position or his life. Were it not that China is so bulky and slow to move, it would have been affected far more than it has been by this powerful factor in its progress. Even as it is, great changes for the better have been made, and greater still are probably impending. Large bodies move slowly. We must not be too impatient to see things progress more rapidly, but be content if there be a continual advance with no retrograde movement. Taking courage from the past, we should hope for more in the future.

Under this head I may mention some other lines of progress in China which, though not directly connected with the Customs service, are the result of the influence of foreign intercourse exerted chiefly, perhaps, through the customs. Arsenals have been constructed at Foochow, Canton, Shanghai, Nankin, etc., and large dockyards and naval depôts established at Port Arthur and Wei Hai Wei, in the gulf of Pechili. These latter, with their fortifications, and the ships which had taken refuge there, have recently been captured by the Japanese. China spent large sums of money on modern guns and ships which she did not know how to manage, and her soldiers and sailors lacked the skill or patriotism to defend. David refused to don Saul's armor because he had not tried it, but the Chinese undertook to use incompetent, unreliable men to work superior arms that they knew not how to handle, or were not brave enough to preserve from the enemy. Still, the fact that they provided themselves with these modern appliances shows their desire and purpose to follow in the wake of European progress in military affairs.

But it is not in the arts of war alone that the Chinese have manifested a wish for improvement. They have also attempted to introduce foreign machinery for manufacturing purposes. In Shanghai, Hankow, Canton, etc., they have factories for making cotton and woolen goods, paper mills, iron foundries, etc. They have also introduced Western mining machinery in their coal mines in Formosa, Kai P'eng, etc., while photography, photo-engraving, electro-plating, electric lighting and other modern arts are in common use in some of the cities open to foreign influence. These points of Western intercourse show that China is beginning to see and value modern progress, and is not slow to adopt those things which she sees are of advantage. Copies of rare and valuable books are reproduced by photo-lithography, and the price of standard works is much lowered, putting within the reach of the many what was formerly the exclusive property of the few. This must tend to increase the intelligence of the race. All these things are in the line of progress, and when Chinese self-conceit is once sufficiently overcome for them to acknowledge their indebtedness to the West for these improvements, will help to remove the feeling of contempt and hostility with which they affect to look down upon everything that does not bear the stamp of Chinese antiquity. As it is now, those who wish to introduce new arts or fresh thoughts among their countrymen, feel too often compelled to resort to the subterfuge of pretending that they are but the restoration of some lost art, or the restatement of some ancient doctrine. Still, some people have enough common sense to see through these pretenses, and are honest enough to feel, if not to acknowledge, that there is something good outside of China.

DIPLOMATIC INTERCOURSE.

Alongside of the influence of the Customs Service, we must place that of the Diplomatic and Consular Services. Though representing their own Governments and not in the employ of the Chinese Government, nor thrown into such intimate daily contact with the Chinese, perhaps, as those who are in the Customs Service, still they occupy positions where they can exert much influence on the most influential class of China. Many of these men, especially those connected with countries which have an organized Consular Service, are able Chinese scholars, often more widely, if not more thoroughly, acquainted with Chinese literature than most of the Chinese literati themselves, and are held in high respect by those with whom they are thrown in frequent contact. Where they are not so thoroughly absorbed in their Chinese studies as to be mere scholars, and forgetful of their position as pioneers of a new civilization which is to uplift China, they may prove powerful factors in its advancement. As a rule they are honorable gentlemen, and the Chinese may get from them ideas of honor and straightforward dealing, very different from those which they find among their own officials. Their decisions are almost always just, and their punishments humane. In almost every point they will compare favorably with the native officials with whom they have to deal. Even where they do not urge schemes for the benefit of the people, the indirect effect of their official lives is almost always beneficial. Those in the ports, as well as those high in authority on the Embassy at Peking, are often in a position to offer valuable advice to the Chinese, and to exert a moral influence when they cannot enforce a political one. Thus this Service is an im-

9

portant factor in the influences which tend to re-construction in China. Backed as they are by the powerful authority of the states which they represent, not only their official acts, but their personal suggestions and advice, carry great influence. Apart from this, their personal character often carries much weight.

CHINESE BAPTIST ACADEMY.—PUPILS.

CHAPTER X.

GOING ABROAD.

ANOTHER reconstructive force that has been powerfully, though it may be, silently, affecting China, is the influence of the Chinese who have gone abroad. If the Chinese have felt the influence of the few foreigners who have lived in their midst, it is not strange that they should be affected by the atmosphere which has surrounded them when dwelling in the midst of foreigners in the lands of the West.

DIPLOMATIC SERVICE.

Two classes of Chinese have gone abroad: those in the embassies who have been sent abroad by the Government, and those who have emigrated of their own accord with the desire to improve their pecuniary condition. The same treaties which gave foreign ambassadors the right to reside in Peking, gave to China the right to send ambassadors to reside in the Capitals of the West. Especially after the Burlingame treaty did China avail herself of this privilege, and appoint ministers and consuls to the West. Though still but few in number, comparatively, they have not been without an important influence on the Chinese Government. Ministers with their attachés and retinue have seen something of the results of Western civilization. They have been impressed by the splendid achievements in architecture and engineering, by the crowded streets, the vast mercantile and manufacturing establishments, and the delicate and useful fabrics of European and American cities. The strong iron bridges, the lofty warehouses, the rapid railway cars, the luxuriously furnished and fast-going steamers, the order and discipline in vast armies and navies, the size, precision, rapid-firing and deadly effect of the fire-arms have all left their impression on their minds. The modes of government and administration, the character of the officials, and the happiness and contentedness of the governed have all been studied, and so the faults and defects in social life and moral character have not gone unnoticed. Perhaps the fact which strikes their materialistic minds most forcibly is the great wealth of Western communities. They are too apt to ascribe all improvement and prosperity to this, and overlook the moral ideas which lie at the basis of our civilization. They say, " If the Chinese only had as much money as the Occidentals, they would have all these

things too." They are apt to ignore the perseverance, the conscientiousness, the love of truth and
accuracy, the enlarged view, the breadth of mind,
and the obedience to law which underlie all these
grand results. They fail to credit with its true
value our constant desire to improve on the past
and break away from conservative traditions—to remember that as long as China persists in *copying*
instead of *inventing*, in worshiping the dead past
instead of pressing onward into the hopeful future,
she can never make any true advancement. No
nation whose golden age is in the past can have any
motive to progress. China gives no weight to
ideas, but merely looks at appearances. Still, new
ideas do break in upon the minds of these Orientals,
and their thoughts are quickened. Hence Marquis
Tseng, one of China's best ministers to Europe,
admitted that China had been asleep, and that her
"Awakening" was only beginning, but he acknowledged the influence of foreign intercourse by
granting that it had succeeded in awaking her.
Some of these ministers have published their diaries
and observations, and these have had their effects
on the thinking men of China. Others of those
who have been in the diplomatic service of China
have no doubt had their tales to tell of what they
have seen in Western lands. Thus the Embassies
to the West have been a factor in China's awakening,

and their good results will be seen still more in the future than they have been in the past. As, one after another, some of China's ablest men have seen Western civilization, they will, on their return, help to dispel those illusions which have been blinding the eyes of the Chinese people.

It is true that hitherto Chinese ambassadors have been attracted only by the material civilization of the West. In compliance with their recommendations, China has lavishly poured out her treasure for Krupp guns and war vessels of modern patterns. What they have failed to see is the importance of the man behind the gun. As it was said with regard to the Franco-German war of 1872, it was not a trial of needle-guns against *chassepots*, but of the men behind the guns, so the Chinese will have to learn that it is to the people—the officers and the rank and file that they must look for success. The men must have confidence in their leaders and must be actuated by a true patriotism. This truth is in accordance with the instructions of their own great sage. When asked about the conditions of prosperity in a state, Confucius said : "There must be a sufficiency of food, a complement of troops, and the full confidence of the people in their rulers." When his disciples inquired as to the relative importance of the three, he said, first, "Take away the troops,"

then, " Take away the food, for from of old men die,
but a people without confidence cannot stand." *
It is just this confidence which is lacking in China.
It is to be hoped that these Chinese scholars who
visit the West will see that there is something
in our Christia ncivilization besides mere material
advancement, that the progress of the individual is a
more important factor in the prosperity of the state
than the use of improved machinery. The Chinese
people have in them the elements of a stalwart civilization ; if developed by the forces of Christianity
there is much to hope for in them in the future. If
they would only put away their self-confidence and
learn to become little children for a while, they might
before long become real men. The basal truth of
Christianity, " Except ye be converted (turn about),
and become as little children," is what they need
for their true advancement

EMIGRATION.

Another class of Chinese who have gone abroad
is the *Emigrants*. The emigration of the Chinese
is not confined to recent times, though it has
naturally greatly increased with the facility of intercourse which is the result of modern commerce.

* Quoted in " China Recorder," Vol. xxvi, No. 1.

The countries about the China Sea are full of
Chinese. By their superior energy and business
ability they have absorbed the trade of these lands,
and pushed into the background the indolent and
shiftless people of these regions.

There are some two and a half millions of Chinese
in Siam out of a total population of eight millions.
In Bankok, the capital of that kingdom, the Chinese
number three hundred thousand in a population of
five hundred thousand. In Singapore, that flourishing British colony in the Straits of Malacca, two-
thirds of the real estate is owned by the Chinese,
and they occupy positions of influence and honor,
some of them being members of the Legislative
Council. Most of the coasting trade on the Ma-
layan peninsula is in the hands of the Chinese,
and they are scattered in all the settlements and plantations on the seaboard. Fifty-five thousand Chinese arrived in Singapore from China in one quarter
—three months. From this center they are distributed to the Dutch and native territories. In the
Spanish city of Manilla on Luzon there are twenty
thousand of them. Most of the artisans in Java are
Chinese. The Chinese form an important part of
the population of the British settlement of North
Borneo. They are found in great numbers in Ran-
goon and in other coast towns of Burma. In Saigon
and the ports of French Cochin China, most of the

trade is carried on by Chinese merchants. Thus the ports around the China Sea, opened up by the prowess and enterprise of European states, have come to be occupied by the Chinese, who are the most progressive element in the Asiatic population. With their enterprise and their wealth they have carried their vices and their evil tendencies; hence gambling, opium-smoking and licentiousness abound wherever they are found.

In the North, too, the energetic, frugal, persevering Chinese are occupying Tartary, and developing and getting control of the trade between China and the Tartar tribes, and also cultivating a trade with Russia. Chinese merchants are also found in Korea and Japan. Enterprising, unscrupulous, untiring and persistent, they are the Jews of Eastern Asia. Traders by instinct, they grow wealthy by accumulating small savings. Polite, accommodating and ever on the alert, they seek to please their customers. Ever ready to pander to the vices of their patrons, their consciences rarely hinder them from accepting the most paltry gains. No wonder then they succeed where others fail.

This contact with their neighbors, north and couth, has had no elevating effect on the Chinese. They have gone as teachers rather than learners; as pioneers of a civilization superior to that of the surrounding nations. Hence this intercourse has had no reconstructive force. It is only as the Chinese have been brought into contact with the Anglo-Saxon race in America and Australia that they have felt the reviving touch of Western Civilization.

God's primal commission to man was : " Be fruitful and multiply ; and replenish the earth and subdue it " (Gen. i. 28). Man's tendency ever has been to become congested in some favored localities.   The first Divine judgment after the flood was intended to counteract this tendency, and men were " scattered abroad," from Babel " upon the face of all the earth " (Gen. xi. 8).   As men scatter seed in order to get a harvest, so God's plan seems to be to develop the waste places of the earth by filling them with men.   Inferior tribes who fail to carry out the command to " subdue " the earth by tilling it and developing its resources are, in the providence of God, supplanted by superior ones; races which are undeveloped or have retrograded are uplifted by being thrown into contact with more energetic, more advanced races.   Gold has often been the great magnet which God has used for attracting men to the unoccupied or sparsely settled parts of our earth. All know how the desire to find the precious metals was the most potent factor in the settling of America.   This was the lode-stone which guided the ships of Columbus and drew forth the expeditions of

SMALL BOAT OR SAMPAN.

Cortez and Pizarro. It was the desire for gold
which led English merchants to fit out costly expeditions; and if the navigators failed to bring back
gold as at least a part of their cargo, they were put
down as unsuccessful, however important their geographical discoveries might have been. It was gold
that brought the Chinese to California and Australia. "Old Gold Hills" and "New Gold Hills"
are the names by which California and Australia
have always been known among the Chinese. When,
after 1849, the tide of emigration towards California
set in, from the Atlantic slope by way of Panama,
and from the Mississippi valley across the plains,
the ear of the Chinese across the Pacific soon caught
the sound of the pickaxes, and visions of yellow
gold flitted across their eyes. The mighty attraction of gold was felt over in Asia, and set the hearts
of the Chinese to throbbing with delight, and led
them to stake their hoarded savings with the hope
of gaining wealth. Nor were they unwelcome.
Content to gather up the fragments, they did not
come into conflict with the claims of others. By
their industry, their patient endurance of toil, their
reliability, their quiet, unassuming lives, they soon
proved to be most valuable as a laboring class, and
their presence was felt to be a needful factor in the
development of the country. As the pioneers began
to settle down and gather their families around

them, the Chinese became invaluable as house-serv-
ants. Quiet, orderly, quick to learn, obedient and
industrious, they made themselves a necessity in the
community. As some accumulated means they became merchants, and contributed largely to develop
a trade between China and the United States. For
some reason many of them took up the laundry-
trade. Probably it was because the work was light,
and they had the foresight to perceive that their
carefulness, regularity, industry, honesty and
patience could be made to pay them well. Some
also set up as cigar-makers and slipper-makers, and
after sewing-machines became common, many of
them ran sewing-machines and did work on overalls
and the coarser kinds of work. When the railroads,
which have done so much for the development of
California, began to be constructed, Chinese contractors took contracts for sections of the roads,
and introduced large numbers of contract laborers
from China. Though unable to do so much hard
work on a stretch as the European navvies, they
proved preferable on many accounts. They were
steadily industrious, were content with lower wages,
did not get drunk and get to fighting, and could
always be counted on for punctuality and steady
work. Europeans, I have been told, after being
paid off on Saturday evening, frequently went off
on a debauch, and did not put in an appearance

until Tuesday, and were then not able to do efficient work. Then they were always ready for a strike when excited by some designing leader, and were not indisposed to relieve the monotony of their toil by taking part in a fight every now and then and letting their work drop meanwhile. Then antagonisms began to arise. The grog-shop keepers who batten on their fellow-men, and ever strive to transfer hard-earned money from the pockets of the toiling laboring man to their own, began to complain that the Chinese did not spend their money in this country, but sent it all abroad. The cry was made that the Chinese were slaves. This is not true. They were contract laborers engaged in China, their passages advanced to them and an outfit provided for them; in return they gave a lien on their earnings. No doubt many of the contractors made much money, but they also took large risks.

With the opening of the Pacific Railroad and the cheapening of steamer fares, a different class of settlers came into California. The laboring classes came, and the competition between Chinese and European labor became more marked. Prejudice against the Chinese increased. Probably a different class of Chinese, too, came in. With the contract laborers, and perhaps among them, came desperate characters, gamblers, men who escaped from justice, and men whose relatives and friends were

10

glad to get rid of them by sending them to California. The Chinese, like other nationalities, insisted on bringing their customs and vices with them. They took advantage of the freedom of our laws to erect heathen temples in our midst, and their idol processions marched through our streets ; they took advantage of the laxity of our police to open opium dens to entice the unwary whites, as well as to enjoy their own favorite dissipation ; they set up their gambling tables, and had their gambling rooms barricaded and fortified so as to resist the raids of the police; they brought over their abandoned women and set up their brothels in country towns as well as in the cities. Some one has said : " If you want to see the reason for our restrictive legislation against the Chinese, you have only to go to Chinatown, in San Francisco." They are no better in many other places. The low, heathenish morals of the Chinese has, no doubt, much to do with the prejudice which exists against the Chinese.

But the labor question is the main factor in the opposition and race-antagonism. Many of those who object to the morality of the Chinese are no better themselves. Substitute whisky for opium, and cards for *fan-tan,* and you have the same evils. There is the same inclination to bribe the police, and the same desire to indulge the lowest tastes and passions. The whites are not without reason at all times when they complain of the Chinese displacing them. Especially does it seem a hardship when Chinese men take the bread out of the mouths of white women and children. I heard of a case in San Francisco which will illustrate this. A Jewish clothing house gave employment to some fifty women and girls, who made garments on sewing machines. A Chinese contractor offered to do the same work for a few cents cheaper a day, and the clothier dismissed the whites, the wives and daughters of laboring men, and gave the job to the Chinamen. The Chinese workmen work on Sunday just as on any other day, and often work until twelve o'clock at night. As they are young men, they have no interruption from family duties, and of course can easily afford to underbid the women. It does seem hard when light work is taken away from women by strong men who should rightfully work in the fields. It is not strange, therefore, that there should be an outcry against Chinese labor. Of course all violent and lawless demonstrations by sandlotters and hoodlums, under the lead of men like Dennis Kearney, are reprehensible and foolish, but the real hardships lend some excuse to the harangues of those who are themselves too lazy to work, but claim to be the special friends of the laboring white men.

The rough treatment which the Chinese receive from the rowdies and baser element of the people,

and the injustice and deceit which are often practiced upon them, must give them a very poor opinion of the white race.   And then, living as the
Chinese do, mostly in the slums of the cities, they
see only the worst examples of our family life; they
mingle almost entirely with the lowest Europeans,
and see little of the pure morality and domestic virtues of a real American home.   A few, however, do
live as servants in Christian families, and many as
laundrymen secure business transactions with refined and kindly disposed people.   The benefits
which accrue to the Chinese from emigration are
mainly from the external fruits of our civilization,
and from the Christian influences exerted by instruction in schools and mission-work for these men
whom God, in His providence, has thrown in our
midst.   Of the latter I will speak more fully hereafter.

The general results of our civilization tend to
make the Chinese realize how far behind they themselves are in the line of civilization and progress.
Our railroads and elevated roads, our magnificent
bridges and buildings, our numerous household conveniences, our waterworks, gas and electric lights,
cable and trolley cars, expensive church buildings
and comfortable houses, public and other schools,
all attract their attention.   When they return to
China I have often heard them remark how dirty

everything there seems compared with the neatness
and cleanliness of America, how slow their antiquated modes of locomotion are, and how little idea
the people seem to have of the value of time. The
slow ways and dirty habits of their own people
seem often to disgust them, and they are seldom
satisfied until they return to America again. They
feel, too, that their property is much safer under
our laws.

In Australia the condition of the Chinese is much
as that in America. They feel the force of the same
race-prejudice and the antagonisms of the labor
question.

The emigration to Siam and the Straits Settlements has been largely from the Fuhkien province,
but numbers of the emigrants were Cantonese. The
emigration to America and Australia has been almost
entirely from the province of Kwang Tung (Canton),
and most of the people are from the neighborhood
of Hong Kong and Macao. A few have gone from
the interior, but most are from districts on or near
the seaboard. These are the people who have been
longest in contact with foreign influence at Canton,
Hong Kong and Macao.

We cannot dismiss the subject of Chinese emigration without noticing the Coolie trade. Though
nominally a system of contract labor it soon, especially in the hands of the Portuguese in Macao, de-

generated into a systematic slave trade.   The Chinese coolie agents, with or without the connivance of their foreign employers, used all the resources of force and cunning to kidnap the unwary country folk.   Young men were promised employment in Hong Kong as artisans and carried to Macao as coolies.   Once in the barracoons there, they were treated as slaves. Though having the opportunity of going through the form of making a legal contract before the authorities, they were so intimidated and so closely guarded by their keepers that they signed contracts to emigrate.   Some, doubtless, went voluntarily, but many went under compulsion, or were deceived into giving consent by all kinds of false promises. Children were enticed and stolen away from their parents.   One of our old Chinese deacons could never read the story of Joseph without breaking down and giving way to his tears, for his oldest son, a boy of fourteen, was stolen away by the coolie agents. I have had mothers come to me for their sons, and wives for their husbands, saying they had been carried away to the foreign ships by force or by fraud.   I have visited these ships, lying at Whampoa, and too often commanded by American captains, and tried in vain to obtain the release of a man; for even though the money claimed to have been advanced might be refunded, the captains are anxious to get their full tale of passengers and set sail as soon as

SEDAN CHAIR.

possible. In some cases regular piracy was practiced by men to secure coolies for Peru. On one occasion a ship appeared before a Chinese town flying signals of distress ; claiming that carpenters were needed on board to stop a leak, and offering them high wages ; as soon as they got the men down the hold they fastened down the hatches and sailed off with their prey. In another case a town was bombarded, and as the inhabitants were fleeing for their lives the men were captured and carried off to the slave-ship. Before long, however, it was found that these violent measures would not pay, for the Chinese, in their recklessness and desperation, set fire to the ships, sacrificing their own lives to take revenge on their captors. In one case all, crew and coolies, were burned to death or drowned. One of these white miscreants was caught in the British colony of Hong Kong, tried and convicted of piracy, but released on some legal technicality, and soon returned to China as consul for one of the South American States! Not all of the coolie trade, however, was of this character. Some was genuine emigration. Those who were kidnapped were sent mostly to Peru and Havana. The British Government sought to regulate the traffic, and has always demanded that all coolies who went to British colonies or in British ships should go under strict Government supervision. By arrangement with the Chinese authorities the traffic was carried on under their inspection and under the control of the British Colonial authorities. Most of the emigration to British Guiana and Mauritius and Trinidad was of this kind.

The coolie trade not unnaturally created much prejudice against foreigners and proved a great hinderance to mission work. Of course it did not tend to give the Chinese any too good an opinion of the men from the West, nor was the influence of those foreigners with whom the coolies were thrown into contact usually very beneficial to them. In British Guiana, however, many of the Chinese have prospered. Much mission work has been done among them, and quite a number became Christians. In this connection I may mention the case of Lough Fook. This young man was converted while a barber's apprentice at Canton, and was baptized by my colleague, Rev. C. W. Galliard. He soon felt a desire to preach and accompanied me on some of my country tours. Before long, he showed that, in addition to his stalwart Christian character, he bid fair to be an effective speaker. After exercising his gifts in preaching for a while, and always refusing to be a paid preacher, preferring to support himself, he became interested in the welfare of his fellow-countrymen who were going in large numbers to Guiana. He finally decided to go out as a coolie under a contract to work for seven years on a sugar plantation. On his voyage out he talked to his fellow emigrants, and after his arrival, began to hold meetings for them on Sunday and on week nights. His work was blessed. Christian friends became interested in him and bought out the last two years of his time that he might devote himself entirely to religious work among his fellow-countrymen. He was set apart to the ministry, baptized a number of Chinese converts, and soon became pastor of a Baptist Church of over 100 members. They were trained to habits of Christian giving, and not only put up their meeting-house and helped their pastor, but were able to send money back to China to aid in the work there. They established two co-operative stores, all the profits of which went towards Christian work in Guiana and in China. After doing efficient work for several years, Brother Lough Fook fell a victim to pulmonary disease and went to be with Christ. Brother Tso Sune converted under Lough Fook's ministry, returned to China and became one of our most reliable native preachers, and served as the efficient pastor at different times of our three principal churches in Canton, Shiu Hing and Tsing Yuen. He also died some two years ago.

Some of the Chinese emigrants to Spanish America acquired a competency and have returned to spend their latter days in comfort in their native land. I have never heard of any who were converted or returned to try and do any religious work among their fellow-countrymen in China.

In speaking of Chinese emigrants we should not omit those who have gone to the Sandwich Islands. These islands are known to the Chinese as the "Sandal Wood Hills," for this fragrant wood (*Santalum Pyrularium*) is much valued in China as one of the constituents of their incense as well as the material from which they make carved boxes, paper-knives, etc. The intercourse between China and these islands has existed for a century, and so many Chinese have settled there that it was stated a few years ago that the Chinese men were more numerous than the native Hawaiian men; of course there are more native women, for few Chinese women emigrate. Some of these have accumulated property and most are thriving. Christian work has been carried on among the Chinese in these islands, and not a few of them were Christians in China before they emigrated to Honolulu.

In connection with Chinese emigration it will be remembered that Christian work for the Chinese was begun among the emigrants in the South before China itself was opened. The early Protestant missionaries, as Medhurst, Milne, Dyer, Abeel, Goddard and Dean, began their work among the Chinese in Batavia, Singapore and Bankok; some of the earliest converts were gathered in from among the Chinese from Fuhkien and Kwang Tung, residing in these ports. Dr. Morrison, it is true, resided in Macao and Canton, but only as a translator to the East India Company, and could not openly work as a missionary. Before the war of 1842 and the subsequent cession of Hong Kong and opening of the five ports, many Roman Catholics, and a few Protestant missionaries resided in the Portuguese settlement of Macao at the western entrance of the Lin Tin Bay, forty miles from Hong Kong, which is at the Eastern entrance. Most of the preliminary mission work was done in the outports. The Anglo-Chinese college was located in Singapore, and Medhurst's Dictionary was published in Batavia. When China was opened most of the work was transferred to Hong Kong and China. Thus the emigrants were among the first to yield their ancient conservatism under the influence of contact with Western influence.

CHAPTER XI.

RECONSTRUCTIVE FORCES.

CHINESE IN THE UNITED STATES.

THE Chinese emigration to America and the fact that Christian influences had been brought to bear upon them have already been alluded to. I wish now to dwell more fully on the latter point.

In the providence of God America seems to be the great caldron where the ingredients of different nationalities are mingled and seething together. Just what the product will be it may be difficult to predict; but we know that unless the true spirit of Christianity makes itself felt the new product will be no improvement on the past. As our ancestors, the English, are the outcome of Anglo-Saxon, Kelt, Dane and Norman mingled in political union, so the American is to be the outcome of mingled races; not necessarily mingled in blood, but feeling influences brought from all quarters. The coming of the Chinese introduced a new element, almost insoluble, into the mass. Hitherto our immigrants had been from Europe, of the same white race as

the original settlers. Added to these were some
from Africa, of an emotional, impressible race,
ready to copy those about them and in a state of
subordination where they were without much social
or political influence. With the influx of the
Chinese came Orientals. Asiatic as to their vices,
but with an energy, industry, persistency, vitality and self-assertiveness like those of the European. It is true, their number was never very
great; never much over one hundred thousand, at
any one time, but the thought of the possible influx
of the numerous hordes of Asia was thought a
menace to our institutions and our civilization.
Politicians sought to check the immigration, and
earnest-minded Christians found themselves con-
fronting the question, "What is God's object in
bringing the quick-witted, intelligent heathen into
our midst?" and saying, "God will surely hold us
'guilty concerning our brother,' if we neglect this
opportunity of trying to stamp the die of Christianity
upon them while they are among us, and to mold
their characters into the image of Christ." Surely
it was the promptings of God's Spirit which led the
Christians of America to try and win the confidence
and respect of those who were so often oppressed and
despised by our fellow-countrymen, and to endeavor
to uplift and help our fellow-men who were debased
by heathenism, ignorance and sin. But how could

they be reached? A great gulf seemed to yawn
between us and them. Clannish and inclined to
keep to themselves, differing from us in habits and
customs, suspicious of the whites, and cherishing a
sense of the wrongs too often inflicted by them, proud
of their own sages and literature, and clinging with
all the tenacity of conservatism to their idolatrous
superstitions, how could they be reached? Then
their language was a great barrier. Knowing no
English except a few words and phrases useful in
their business, speaking what they did know in an
almost unintelligible, miserably broken English, there
seemed to be an insuperable barrier to getting any
religious truth into contact with their prejudiced,
untaught minds. It may have occurred to some to
distribute Chinese gospels and tracts among them,
but here came up another difficulty. Many of them
can read very little, and are not prepared to comprehend the new truths of Christianity, and, worse
than this, most of them have no desire to learn
Christian truth and care nothing for the religion of
the race who so frequently look down upon them
and wrong them. There were but two ways open.
One was to have returned missionaries who had
learned the language try to give them the Gospel;
the other was to try to reach them by means of
the English language, to try and persuade the
Chinese to learn the language of spiritual truth as

CHINESE BAPTIST ACADEMY.—TEACHERS AND MANAGERS.

they or others had picked up what they needed for the business intercourse of common life. This was a task indeed, and yet Christian men and women were found who had the faith and perseverance to undertake it.

To speak first of what was last in point of time, the Chinese Sunday school has become the most widely spread means of teaching our religion to the Chinese. The plan owes its adoption mainly to Reverend Otis Gibson, a Methodist returned missionary who was laboring among the Chinese in California. The idea soon spread, and most Protestant denominations had one or more Sunday schools for the Chinese in the chief cities and towns of the Pacific coast. There was much opposition manifested at first by the people who hated the Chinese and dreaded their knowing more of the English language. The Methodist church in San José was burned to the ground soon after a Chinese school was opened there. Threats were made in other places. Still the work went on, until now there are Chinese Sunday schools in almost every city of the United States where Chinese are to be found. The Chinese came to these schools primarily not to learn religion but the English language ; they wished for help for their trade and not for their souls. Yet God's revealed truth had a power, especially when backed by the faithful, earnest prayers of those who

taught it.   Learning only for an hour and but once
a week, of course the progress of the pupils in learning the rudiments of the language would be slow,
and it would be some time before they could read
the Bible so as to get any idea of its meaning.
They were impressed more by the kindness and
patience and unrequited efforts of their teachers
than by the truths which the teachers strove to inculcate.   Still the persevering efforts of godly men
and women were not without result.   Some of the
scholars began to pray for themselves and were converted, and much real good to the cause of Christ
has come from these schools.

Nothing human is perfect, and it is not surprising
that mistakes were made, and abuses crept in, in connection with some of these schools.   The teachers
were ignorant of the Chinese character, and suffered
their sympathies to carry them too far.   Designing
Chinese sought to work upon the feelings of their
teachers, in order to get their aid in lawsuits.   The
fact that the Chinese were often unjustly accused
and failed to secure their rights in our courts led
many sympathetic teachers to interest themselves in
cases where their pupils were in the wrong.   This
led the heathen Chinese to hate the churches and
schools, and many honest men among them to refuse
to have anything to do with them.   Undue familiar-
ities were sometimes allowed by thoughtless girls

who were unwisely permitted to act as teachers. The respectable Chinamen look upon any mingling of the sexes as reprehensible, and being unable to understand the greater freedom allowed by our customs, looked upon all intimate conversation between a pupil and a female teacher, especially a young one, as dangerous to morality. Too great familiarity was permitted, and in some cases the teachers were even foolish enough to marry their pupils. This of course excited all the race-feeling of the white community. Some schools have been entirely broken up where such a case occurred, and the woman's happiness for life is generally blighted. Then some teachers have petted their pupils, so that they have grown so self-conceited as to excite the contempt of their fellow-countrymen, and when they return to China they wilt at once under opposition, or become nuisances in the native churches, because they do not get the foolish attentions which were paid to them in America. Nothing takes the backbone and manliness out of a Chinaman, or any other man, like petting.

Then the Christian name has suffered among the Chinese by the churches hastily receiving unconverted men. The pupils sometimes make a profession of religion merely to please their teachers and show their appreciation of the kindness they have received. Their fellow-countrymen who know their daily lives have no respect for them nor the religion they profess.   Scandals have arisen, too, from the giving and receiving of presents.   The Chinese are anxious to show their appreciation of the gratuitous instruction they receive and the kindness shown them by making presents to their teachers.   In some cases costly presents have been expected and even requested by thoughtless teachers. This has led the Chinese to misapprehend the motives of their instructors, or what should be the motives of all who engage in Christian work, and suppose that they teach merely for gain.   It would be well if teachers would decline any valuable presents and only accept those of a smaller value as tokens of the pupils' appreciation of their kindness in teaching them.

It is not surprising that mistakes have been made, the only thing surprising is that some people never seem to learn their mistakes.   I believe, however, that in the great majority of schools, there is much improvement, and that experience, the best of teachers, is teaching wisdom.   Where properly conducted, I see no reason to decry this form of Christian effort, but on the contrary, I believe that God's people would fail to secure His blessing if we permit these strangers to dwell in our midst for years and make no effort to teach and to save them.   Whatever may be said of African slavery as it existed in

our midst, it cannot be said that the religious needs
of the slaves were neglected; hence we see large
numbers of that race brought to our shores as
heathen now ranged among the professed followers
of our Lord Jesus Christ, and Christ-like characters
developed in many of them. Surely the same love
for souls and desire for the glory of God should
lead us to work equally for the salvation of the
Chinaman as for that of the negro.

As to the results of the work among the Chinese,
experience shows that the efforts of God's people
here have not been in vain. While in some cases
those who have professed Christianity here have
proved recreant, and have disappointed the hopes
of those who were interested in their spiritual welfare, others have proved true, and have been help-
ful to the mission work in China. It is a very
severe test that the young men have to endure who
go from this country, especially if they have been
petted here, to their homes in the midst of heathenism. Parents and those in authority over them
ridicule and oppose them, and leave no art untried
and few forms of force unattempted, to compel them
to abjure Christianity and to return to the worship of
idols and of their ancestors. They have no concep-
tion of a conscientious adherence to conviction, but regard all Christian firmness as contumacy, and a rebellion against the commands of their superiors. The

strongest kind of pressure is brought to bear upon
the new convert, and it is not strange that, being
the only Christian, perhaps, in his town or village,
he sometimes yields.   Many, however, have been as
gold tried in the fire, and have passed through the
fiery ordeal unscathed.   Some grow cold and half-
hearted, without actually going back from their religion.   Some come out of the fire all the brighter.
Not a few of our best preachers in South China have
been converted in this country.   Then they often
have a push and energy, an intelligent understanding
of the methods of Christian work, and a realization
of the miserable condition of their fellow-countrymen
beyond that of those who have never been out of
China.   They seem to have caught some of the fire
and fervor that prevail in our favored land, and so
prove a quickening and uplifting force in our native
churches.   Brother Ch'an Kum Sing, converted in
New York, and recently called to his heavenly home,
was one of the most devout, self-denying, earnest, con-
sistent Christians I have ever known in any land.
He has left his impress on the work in China, and
his straightforward, downright Christian character
has had an influence upon our native Christians
that will not soon be effaced.   The men converted
in America, though often not without their faults,
form an active, progressive element among our
native members, and are more inclined to break

with the ancient conservatism than many of those who have never breathed the freer air of America. So those who are working for the religious welfare of the Chinese in America through the means of the English language, have no reason to be discouraged, but may be cheered by the thought that they are contributing their quota towards the winning of China for Christ.

As to the other branch of the work, reaching the Chinese, here through means of their own language, it has been carried on chiefly on the Pacific Slope. About 1854, Rev. J. L. Shuck, who had been a missionary in China for some twenty years, was sent to California by the Southern Baptists to begin a work among the Chinese immigrants there. He began a successful work in Sacramento, where he built a neat little chapel and baptized a number of converts. About the same time, Rev. Mr. Speer was sent out by the Presbyterian Board to San Francisco, and commenced a work there among the Chinese which was continued by Rev. A. W. Loomis and others, and still exists in a flourishing state. The Methodists subsequently carried on a similar work under Rev. Messrs. Gibson and Masters. Chinese preachers were raised up in this country or came over from China to assist in the work. Some of these are now found also in the cities further east, and are doing a good work among their fellow-countrymen. Chinese churches have been organized in California and Oregon, and perhaps elsewhere. These converts have shown a commendable spirit of liberality, and contribute for Christian enterprises in this country as well as send money to China for the evangelization of their native land. Thus Christianity is leavening the masses in Asia by means of the Chinese converts in America, and the teaching given here becomes one of the reconstructive forces at work in China.

The discussion of Chinese Immigration seems to demand some reference to the restrictive legislation against the Chinese in America. This legislation is not peculiar to the United States. The laws in the Australian colonies of Great Britain are in some regards more severe. Not only have shipmasters to pay a large penalty for bringing passengers from China to some of the colonies, but a heavy fine is imposed on Chinese who move from one colony to another. Fifty dollars has to be paid by every Chinaman who lands in British Columbia. The motives for this restrictive emigration are everywhere the same; the Chinese are regarded as an undesirable class of immigrants, because they come into competition with white labor, because they do not bring their families and come as permanent settlers, and because they will bring with them many of the vices and everything that is objection-

FOREIGN SETTLEMENT AND CHINESE TOWN.—CANTON.

able in their heathenism. Polygamy, gambling, opium-smoking and general laxity of morals characterize them wherever they congregate in "Chinatowns" or separate settlements in the cities, while a disposition to form an "*imperium in imperio*," and to regulate their affairs in disregard to the laws of the country, makes them in many cases a source of danger and of suspicion. Then, much of this legislation is based on a scare, and unfounded apprehension as to the influx of immense hordes of Asiatics. While it is not strange that some restrictions should be attempted, yet this legislation has been fitful and often unjust.

By the treaty of 1868, it was agreed that "The United States of America and the Emperor of China cordially recognize the inherent and inalienable right of man to change his home and allegiance, and also the mutual advantage of the free migration and emigration of their citizens and subjects respectively from the one country to the other for the purpose of curiosity, of trade, or as permanent residents."—*Treaty with China, proclaimed July 28th, 1868.*

Availing themselves of this understanding, which has all the force of a compact, the Chinese came to the United States. If our Government found reasons to recede from this action they should have sought a revision of the treaty, which they did do, but before taking this action Congress passed laws, going into almost immediate effect, forbidding such migration. Thus, under the operation of the Scott Act, Chinese passengers who had left for America before the law was passed were not permitted to land, but had to pay their passage back to China. This was an injustice. We have treated China, not as we would have treated a European power, but rather as we have too often been accustomed to treat our Indian tribes—break our obligations when it suited our convenience to do so. It is to be feared that the "Century of Dishonor" has not yet become an anachronism.

The Chinese Government has no desire to see its subjects leave their native land. According to their traditions it is a dishonor to a state to have its people desire to emigrate, (it is like "rats forsaking a sinking ship "). What they do object to, is that their people when just as law-abiding and useful an element in a community as any others should be discriminated against and singled out, when people of other nationalities give us more trouble and are a greater menace to public peace. When it is remembered how we foreigners are discriminated against in China, how our right to reside outside the open ports is denied or disputed, how we are required to carry passports whenever we leave our places of residence, how we are not allowed to acquire real estate, and subjected to many inconveniences, the Chinese have no right to complain of their treatment by the law here, still, we claim to be a country where greater freedom reigns and pride ourselves on our more liberal and advanced civilization and Christian sentiment. It must be admitted that our changeable and restrictive legislation, by its want of fairness and by its injustice, has not tended to raise us in the estimation of the Chinese, and to that extent has hindered our influence as a nation in being a force for uplifting the Chinese, and promoting progress among them.

CHAPTER XII.

RECONSTRUCTIVE FORCES—CONTINUED.

THE WAR BETWEEN CHINA AND JAPAN.

WAR has already been alluded to as a prelude to almost all the changes that have taken place in China. I wish here to speak of the war now waging between China and Japan, as this will probably be the cause of still greater changes in the future. This war has many interesting aspects. To the Christian it presents the unique fact of the two last pagan empires left on earth engaged in deadly conflict. It is not given to us to fathom God's purposes, but this war arose so suddenly, has progressed so rapidly, with all the advantages on one side, and is likely to be followed by such important consequences, that one cannot help feeling that the Providence of God has some special design in permitting it. To the politicians, its most striking feature is the unexpected advent of a vigorous Asiatic Power on the political arena, one that must be taken account of in all our calculations as to the balance of power on the Pacific, and the settlement of the present-day Eastern

Question. We see an Island Empire, occupying a position in Asia as to geography and climate corresponding to that of the British Isles in Europe, with a population exceeding that of Great Britain (40,000,-000 to 26,000,000), a people patriotic, progressive and aspiring, taking and claiming a place among the Powers of the East, similar to that of Great Britain in the West. To the Chinese statesman, whose past efforts have been directed to resisting the encroachments of Russia, or warding off the influence of other European powers, a new bugbear has loomed up and everything will have to be readjusted to the new conditions. The defeat has been a most humiliating one to China. An intelligent Chinaman, a graduate of one of our American colleges, said to me lately: " I wish some first-class European power had given China a good thrashing; there is no hope for any progress without it, but that these little Japs should whip us so ! really it is too bad." That the " dwarfs," as the Chinese contemptuously term the Japanese, should defeat them in every engagement, on sea or on land, is something that must set the most stolid mandarin to thinking. That Japan, with one-tenth of the population and resources, with soldiers of an inferior physique, and without the aid of any European Power, should so quickly and so completely defeat all the forces sent against her, capture two strongholds considered impregnable, and seize the

12

Chinese navy and appropriate it to her own use, is a fact startling enough to arouse the Chinese. It has been like a contest between a sword-fish and a whale; the great, cumbrous thing lying completely at the mercy of its active and vigorous adversary. It has been a contest between progress and conservatism. The Chinese with their gongs and drums, their waving flags,* and their gay jackets with flaring circles right over their breasts and backs, proved excellent targets for the soldiers of Japan as they moved on noiselessly and resistlessly in serried ranks, led by trained and able officers. The patriotic ardor of the islanders as they pressed forward ready to sacrifice their lives for their country, engaged in what they proclaimed from the beginning " a righteous war," contrasted very markedly with the apathy of the Chinese, who felt little interest in the conflict, and less confidence in their unskilled officers, leading them forward to be butchered like sheep. Personally, many of the Chinese are not cowardly; if engaged in a conflict in which their hearts are enlisted, and led by leaders whom they have reason to trust, they will sell their lives as dearly as possible and die rather than yield. In this war the odds were all against them. They were fighting for a preponderating Chinese influence in Korea, about which they

* A consul told me he counted the flags of a body of Chinese troops and found they had one to every two and a-half men !

cared nothing ; they were led by incompetent men ; even when armed with modern arms of precision they knew little about their use.   Then the Japanese had their hospitals and ambulance corps, while the Chinese took no care of their wounded.   The Japanese had an organized commissariat and paid the country people for what was brought them, while the Chinese raided their own countrymen, and were more dreaded by them than their nominal enemies.   The Japanese commander urged his troops to remember that they were warring against the Chinese Government, and not against the Chinese people, whose rights they were ordered to respect, while the Chinese treated their own people as if they were enemies.   The heathenism of old Japan broke forth at Port Arthur, where they ruthlessly massacred both soldiers and citizens, but with this exception they seem to have acted in a civilized way.

Not only have they shown their civilization by manifesting an interest in the physical welfare of their soldiers, but they have also been considerate for their religious welfare.   High Japanese officials have permitted the free distribution of the Sacred Scriptures among the soldiers in the army, and even among those of the Imperial Guard.   They have even gone further and appointed Christian chaplains to the troops who have gone to China, giving them the rations and transportation of captains in the service.   All these things show how progressive the impetuous Japanese are.   They will not be satisfied unless the result of this war be that China shall introduce reforms ; that "stagnant, false, rotten China be taught a lesson it will not forget—a lesson which will start it upon the path Japan has followed so successfully."   The Japanese regard the weakness of China as a menace to all the East, and would fain have her as an ally to resist European aggression in Eastern Asia.

The Chinese were unprepared for the war.   It never entered into the heads of their self-sufficient, arrogant rulers that a little country of little men would ever have the impudence to fight with the venerable empire of China.   Their self-confidence has proved their ruin.   The pride which goes before a fall has led them astray.   They thought that because they had a stronger navy than Japan, had their strongholds at Port Arthur and Wei-Hai-Wei, protected by forts constructed by European engineers, and armed with Krupp guns, that their insignificant neighbors would never venture to attack them.   They probably now begin to see how shortsighted their policy was when they withdrew their students from America.   At the same time that Japan was sending her young men to Europe and America to learn the science and arts of the West, China sent a company of students to America.   A

CANTON CITY WALLS WITH FIVE STORY WATCH-TOWER.

few became Christians, and some cut off their queues, and those who returned to China showed such progressive ideas, that China, like some poor old grandmother, became frightened and recalled her students. Those returned found that all avenues to preferment were closed to them, and no career invited them to continue their studies. To be of any influence in China they must go back to composing stilted essays and repeating time-worn sayings. It is possible that the results of this war may show the Chinese the importance of those studies which they have despised, and the necessity of placing in positions of influence and authority men who are up to the times.

ORIGIN.

To understand the origin of the present war between China and Japan, about Korea, we must go back to the history of the three nations. Korea, as all know, is a peninsula, jutting down from Tartary, between China and Japan. It has an area about equal to that of Great Britain, and a population estimated in 1889, at 10,518,937. The country is mountainous with quite fertile valleys, and is rich in mineral products, embracing the precious metals. It was colonized in early times by the Chinese, and was known to them as the Eastern Kingdom. From

before the Christian era to the tenth century, it was
divided into three states, often warring with each
other.   Japan received her Chinese civilization, not
directly, but through Korea; and the basis of
Japanese arts and handicraft is known.   The Japanese settled at Fu San, on the eastern coast, and
invaded Korea in the third century.   In 1231 the
Mongols invaded it, and in 1256 reduced it to
vassalage to China.   The Koreans having cast off
their allegiance, a Chinese army was sent against
them by the Mings (1368–1644), and the present
Korean dynasty was set up by the Chinese.   In
1597 the Japanese invaded Korea, and after much
fighting, the Chinese and Koreans had a severe
engagement with the Japanese at Ping Yang, the
same place in which the recent battle was fought
by the same combatants.   After this the Japanese
were successful in a bloody and hard-fought battle,
and Korea became tributary to Japan.   In 1636
the Manchus invaded Korea before they secured the
throne of China.   Thus for years, as has been well
remarked, Korea was as the grist between the upper
and nether millstones of Japan and China.   In recent
years, after the United States, England, Russia,
France, and Germany, had tried in vain to open up
Korea and form a treaty, Japan prepared to go
to war with her to revenge any insult offered
to her flag.   China gave Japan a written dis-

claimer of all authority over Korea, and the Japanese succeeded in gaining a " brain-victory " without any fighting, and a treaty was signed Feb. 27th, 1876, opening the ports of Fu San and Gensan, to Japanese trade. In 1882 a few ports were opened to the United States, England, France, and Germany. Then there was an uprising of the conservative Koreans, who put to death the queen, her son, and the ministers, and drove out the Japanese. China renewed her claim to suzerainty and occupied Korea with her troops. The Japanese, however, subdued the insurgents and received compensation for her losses. Thus the battle has raged between the conservatives, aided by China, and the progressive leaders under the influence of Japan. The " Hermit nation," as Korea is termed, still clings to her policy of seclusion, and would gladly exclude other nations, but she cannot hold herself aloof, and her territory has become the fighting ground for the conservative and progressive forces represented by China and Japan. The present conflict was precipitated by a rising of the *Tong Hak,* or native Korean party. Japan and China both sent troops and the jealousies of years broke into open conflict. Japan professes to be the champion of the independence of Korea, while China maintained that it was a subject state. The Koreans are more nearly allied to the Japanese by their language and customs, but the ruling classes are very much in sympathy with China and all that is conservative. All admit that the country is horribly governed, and the people are ground down to the dust by the tyranny and rapacity of their rulers. The Japanese are trying to introduce reforms, and have the sympathies of the enlightened nations of the world in this effort. Japanese interests are predominant there, as most of the trade is in their hands. As Japan stands for the independence and improvement of Korea, most Occidentals will rejoice in her success.

As to the outcome of the struggle, all know how so far the Japanese have won victory after victory, and are now complete masters of the situation. China has sent an embassy to Europe to plead with the Western Powers to intervene and intercede for her, and after much dilly-dallying has deputed Li Hung Chang as her plenipotentiary to Japan to arrange for conditions of peace. The basis of peace is said to be the acknowledgment of the independence of Korea, the session of the island of Formosa to Japan, an indemnity of $250,000,000 gold, the withdrawal of Chinese exterritoriality in Japan, and the stipulation that Japan is to retain possession of the Chinese strongholds of Port Arthur, and Wei-Hai-Wei for a number of years. These conditions, while they can scarcely be termed hard, are very humiliating to China. The war party is in the accendant in Japan, and they will scarcely be satisfied with anything less than the capture of Peking, and the complete humiliation of China. It will be a wiser policy for the Japanese not to be too exacting, for China's resources are so much greater that if she be led to cherish feelings of revenge she will make preparations through long years to resent the humiliation inflicted upon her. China moves slowly but surely.

What effect is this war to have on the future condition of China? One cannot help feeling that there is some important Providential Design in this eventful conflict. It certainly is a most striking fact that in the end of this century our Christian civilization should, after having followed the course of the sun from East to West, at last come into a hand-to-hand conflict with old-world conservatism on the Eastern coast of Asia ; that the impulse which arose in Western Asia should, after sweeping around the world, come into clash with the Oriental heathen form of civilization on the Western shores of the Pacific ; that two Asiatic powers should fight this battle. It can scarcely be doubted that great changes are impending in China. Either she will yield to the force of the shock and open her gates to progress and Christianity, or she will sullenly and stubbornly cling to her idols and perish through disintegration and European intervention and the division of her territory. Oh, that she would be wise and consider her latter end ! Would that she would realize the truth, so consonant with the teachings of her sages, that she must begin with her *men* if she would make any real progress, that *character* underlies all true advancement. Destructive as this war has been to China's army and navy, to her self-esteem and to her long-cherished conservatism, may we not hope that it may prove one of the most effective reconstructive forces that are at work in China, that the rude awakening may arouse her to a sense of her real weakness, and be an impulse in the direction of reform and true progress?

It must be humiliating to China to feel that she has no exterritorial rights in Japan, while the Japanese are to have these rights in China ; that a Chinaman residing in Japan is to be tried before Japanese courts, but a Japanese living in China is subject only to his own Consular courts. By the new treaties with Japan, the Western nations have agreed that, after the year 1900, foreigners living in Japan are to be subject to the decisions of the Japanese courts, and not as now to their own consuls. This privilege is not accorded to China. The reason is plain ; Japan has conformed her legal procedure to Western models, while China allows no jury, permits torture and retains a treatment of prisoners that is simply barbarous. Of course Western nations are not willing, nor is Japan willing, to permit their subjects or citizens to be subjected to a treatment so much more harsh than Chinese offenders would be exposed to in Western lands. It is most humiliating to China to feel that she is looked down upon as still a barbarous state as far as her courts are concerned, and yet this is the fact. She will probably be led by her own feeling of self-respect to introduce reforms, so that other nations will be willing to commit their subjects to her jurisdiction. She must build well lighted, healthful prisons instead of the horrible holes in which her prisoners may be incarcerated now; she must learn to treat a man as innocent until he is proved guilty, to abolish torture as a means of arriving at the proof of guilt, and generally to conform her modes of procedure and of punishment to those adopted in other lands, before other nations will allow her the right to try their subjects before her courts.

So with regard to her army and navy, China must feel the importance of an entire reorganization after Western models. Lord Wolseley, in a recent magazine article, claims that China will never take her rightful place among the nations of the earth until her army is reorganized and the profession of arms be acknowledged as an honorable one. The reverses which have attended her arms during the present war will probably arouse China to make great changes, especially perhaps in educating a class of men for officers. Her present system of securing military graduates is, at most, a system of gymnastics. Archery, lifting heavy weights, and brandishing enormous battle-axes are the exercises through which men pass to attain a military degree. While these develop men physically, they give them no training in the real art of war. All the skill they attain to must be learned on the battle-field. The Chinese will probably be led to see the necessity of having military colleges, of making the service attractive to one who wishes to enter it as a career, by having a system of promotions according to merit, and of pensions for men disabled in the service from wounds or old age.

Probably no event has tended more to put China back than the issue of the brief hostilities with France in 1884, during the war in Cochin China. Though the Chinese fleet was destroyed by the French, the fighting on the border of Anam was indecisive, and peace was concluded. The almost universal opinion of the Chinese is that they obliged France to sue for peace. This opinion, so flattering to Chinese self-esteem, that they had defeated one of the great Powers of Europe, at once took possession of the minds of the people and was fostered to the utmost by the ruling classes. The foreign-

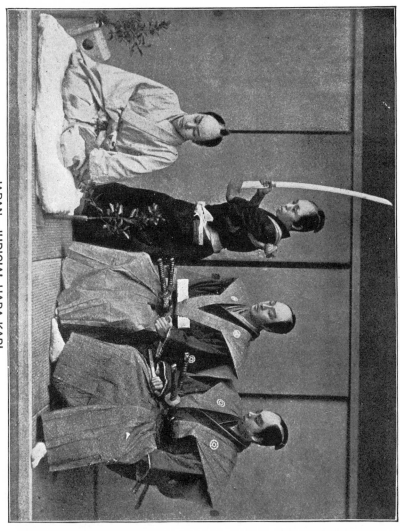

JAPAN.—JUDICIAL HARA-KARI.

ers were tolerated before, but now a spirit of exclu-
sionism sprang up and efforts to crowd them out
became a part of the real policy of China's
rulers. As the Chinese troops won some successes
against the French on the borders of Anam, and, as
they boastingly claimed, were about to wipe them
out, when peace was concluded at Peking, it was
inferred that the Chinese levies armed with European guns were a match for the disciplined troops of
the West. It can easily be seen how the results of
this war, wrested by self-conceit, should tend to make
the Chinese feel satisfied with their present system
of army organization. As General Gordon, " Chinese
Gordon," as he is often called, has pointed out, the
Chinese have some good points as soldiers ;—they
are brave when well led, content with simple food
and can move rapidly, requiring very little baggage.
What they need is efficient organization under com-
petent leaders. The native Chinese officers are ex-
cessively particular about punctilios of etiquette and
gladly receive salutes to which they are not entitled
by their rank. Probably more powder is consumed
in a year in salutes from Chinese gun-boats than
would be expended in a year's campaign against
an enemy, and more cloth employed in making the
flags for a regiment than would be needed for their
coats. The English captain of a Chinese gun-boat
told me that the Chinese commanders were ac-

customed to order the most excessive salutes to be fired for even petty mandarins and especially for those into whose good graces they wished to ingratiate themselves. This obsequiousness is but a common form of Chinese politeness. Until the Chinese officers learn to put aside their arrogance and love of displaying their authority they will never get the services of self-respecting European or American officers to aid them in the work of reconstruction. It is well known that Admiral Lang, an English naval officer in command of the Chinese fleet, resigned because one of the Chinese mandarins, in order to show off in some naval maneuver, usurped authority which belonged to the English commander. A Chinese officer generally thinks more of his rank than of his efficiency, and esteems show more than real merit. These defects must be remedied if the Chinese army and navy are ever to be raised to real efficiency.

If the humiliation resulting from the war with Japan will lead to a reorganization of the courts and army and navy, we may hope it may yet prove a benefit to China. But what she needs most of all is a reorganization in the character of her people. Nothing but Christian truth can accomplish this. Until the *men* of China learn to be less boastful and self-conceited, more truth-loving and sincere, more thoughtful of moral character than of rules of formal politeness, we can never hope for real, thorough progress in China.

CHAPTER XIII.

RECONSTRUCTIVE FORCES—CONTINUED.

EDUCATION.

WE must reckon Christian Education among the most important Reconstructive Forces in China. From of old the Chinese have held education in the highest esteem. Some of their views on the subject are worthy of attention, but there is great room for improvement in their practical methods. They say that the education of a child begins before its birth; that the " women of ancient times in every movement had regard to its effect on the character of their offspring." Their ancient books also speak of the advantage of " changing their sons," i. e. of a father's giving the care and training of a son to a teacher. Schools were begun in early times. There still exists in Peking the almost defunct representative of an institution begun in the Chow dynasty, a thousand years before the Christian era. It retains the same name, " School for the Sons of the Empire," and is still an Imperial institution, supported by the Government. " It was in its glory before the light of science dawned on Greece, and when Pythagoras and Plato were pumping their secrets from the priests of Heliopolis. And it still exists, but it is only an embodiment of ' life in death;' its halls are tombs, and its officers are living mummies." * It was established to instruct the " Sons of the State " in sciences and arts—i. e. in arithmetic, writing, music, archery, horsemanship and ritual ceremonies. It was intended, not as a common school, but an institution to train the sons of the nobility for Government service. From this beginning has been developed the present system of triennial Government examinations, alluded to in a previous chapter, and throughout the centuries attention has been paid to the training of the youth of China.

The teacher occupies a very high place in the estimation of the Chinese. He is exalted to a position of almost idolatrous homage. The name " teacher " is inscribed on a tablet in connection with heaven, earth, prince, and parents as one of the five chief objects of veneration, and worshiped with solemn rites. He is regarded as one whose duty it is to do more than simply impart mental knowledge. He is to be the " instructor, guide, and friend " to his pupil, to be the model on which his morals and manners are to be formed. The per-

* Dr. W. A. P. Martin, " The Chinese," p. 85.

sonal character of the teacher is regarded as of the first importance, and his ability to inspire the pupil with ardor in the pursuit of virtue as the gauge of his efficiency. This is the ideal of the teacher and his office. Of course many come far below this ideal. They are opium-smokers, mere martinets, with no real desire for the moral improvement of their pupils, or utterly careless, permitting the boys to use the foulest language in their presence, and caring for nothing except to secure the patronage of their patrons by putting the scholars through their daily tasks. There are many, however, who take a real interest in the intellectual progress of the boys, and feel some interest in their moral welfare.

When we consider the high estimation in which education is held by the Chinese and the influential position they accord to a teacher, we can easily understand how Christian missionaries would endeavor to utilize these sentiments for the spread of Christianity and the glory of the Lord Jesus Christ. We feel that we have truths of far more importance than the inanities they teach, and that the many valuable moral instructions their books contain should be supplemented by the priceless religious and spiritual truths we have received through God's revealed word. It is felt, too, when we consider how far short the great mass of the Chinese teachers come of their own ideal, that the youth of China should be brought under the influence of characters molded into the likeness of that of Christ—Christian teachers who feel an earnest and prayerful interest in building up the characters of those under their charge.

The Chinese Classics are not lacking in lofty *ideals*. This is something. They compare favorably in their moral teachings with the Greek and Latin classics which are studied in our schools. But as has been well said : "Confucian scholars seem to think that, by paying a sentimental reverence to the instructions of the sages, they have themselves, in some way, become partakers of their virtues." * They have the "knowledge which puffeth up," without the "love that buildeth up." There is no power of the fear of God or true love to man to enforce the sentiments they admire from a distance. The same writer quoted above, says, with truth : "The careful observer of Chinese social life is about equally impressed with the correctness of the moral maxims that are heard from the lips of the people, and with their disregard of such maxims in actual life." The Chinese need a new force to make their high ideals and moral maxims of practical power in the daily life. This can come only from Christian education in its broadest sense.

* Dr. D. Z. Sheffield, in "Records of Shanghai Conference."

So with regard to Western science, Christianity is needed to give the Chinese a true philosophy of the physical universe. The Chinese, though placing Western science far below their own classics, yet are as ready to welcome it as they have been to purchase foreign arms; this is true at least with regard to the more advanced thinkers. The Government has employed Western scholars to translate into Chinese some of the elementary and even advanced works on Astronomy, Botany, Mathematics, Chemistry, Electricity, Engineering, etc., and have admitted some of these branches as subsidiary studies in the examinations. All know that the trend of many of the scientific works of late years has been to exalt Law above the Lawgiver, to deny that there is an Infinite Author of the Universe, or to relegate Him to the region of the unknown or unknowable. This just corresponds with Chinese theories. " If Western philosophy and science come to China divorced from Christianity, Confucian scholars will accept the new learning with proud self-complacency, and will find in it only a confirmation, and a more elaborate illustration of the teachings of Confucian scholars for the last two thousand years. But Western science and philosophy, as taught by Christian men, will be made to give the most convincing testimony to God in nature, in history and in providence." It is an encouraging fact that most, if not all, of the translations alluded to have been made by men who have a reverence for the Word of God, and feel an interest in the religious as well as the intellectual progress of the Chinese. But of course books published under the auspices of the Chinese Government cannot be so distinctively Christian as instruction given in Mission schools. The study of God's works, conducted by men of devout minds, will always prove among the most important evidences of Christianity. Hence the place of Western science in Christian schools.

Christian instruction is needed to lead the Chinese to see the true aim of education. Political preferment, with the consequent gain of emolument and power, is the great aim of Chinese scholars. Though some do enjoy their own literature probably, still there are few who study it for its own sake. There are no grand poems that men will pore over as we do over Homer, Virgil or Shakespeare. The sages taught the principles of government and social relations, and the Chinese mind runs very much in this direction. They do have light verses and abstruse philosophical speculations, but the mass of students think only of such subjects as will enable them to pass the examinations. Christianity is needed to teach men to cultivate their God-given powers with a reference to improving their characters as those who must give an account to God,

BUDDHIST HEAD PRIEST AND ASSISTANT.

and to benefiting their fellow-men. Official employment and not personal virtue is the great object
of the ambition of the Chinese student. The object of Christian instruction is to infuse a higher
motive, and to lead men to live not for self but for
God. Apart from Christianity, Western education
will no more accomplish this object than Chinese
education will. What is needed is the Christian
teacher, realizing the importance of his high vocation, not only to develop the minds of his pupils,
but to influence their wills and elevate their characters.

Christian schools are needed in order that the
advantages of education may be offered to all. It
is the glory of the Chinese system of Government
examinations that every man of talent, however
humble, may have an opportunity of obtaining rank
and office. But no notice is taken of the average
youth, and the females are neglected altogether.
No effort is made to train the great mass of the
people as such. On the contrary, the literary class
look down upon the unlettered masses with all the
arrogance they would feel if they belonged to
another caste, as in India. It remains for Christianity to regard men as men—to try and extend the
opportunities of education to all. Girls' schools as
well as boys' schools have been opened; the ignorant village children, as well as those who live in

the cities, have been gathered in.   Free schools are opened that even the poorest may attend.

Again, Christian schools are needed in order to teach the Bible.   Of late years especially, many of our American colleges have been introducing the systematic study of the Bible as a part of their curriculum.   We have been studying the classics of Greece and Rome for the beauties of expression, and neglecting the great Classic with all its wealth of thought.   Mission schools make the Bible the great text-book.   They are often, in fact, Sunday schools, carried on during every day in the week. Of course the pupils are taught to write their own language, and some of their own school-books are used in learning their own language, but from the first they study Christian books, learn Christian hymns, and are examined in their knowledge of the Bible truths.   Apart from mathematics and the physical sciences, almost all needed mental training may be obtained from the Bible.   The clear reasoning of Paul, the flowing, historical style of the narrative portions, and the lyrical beauty and sublime poetry of psalmist and prophet, make these writings a text-book of rhetoric and logic.   But it is chiefly in its moral and religious truths that the value of the Bible is found.   The Chinese expect a classic to teach virtue and morality, and the Bible comes nearer to their ideas of what a text-book should be than our Western treatises on science do. Of course, Government schools, even those of the English colony of Hong Kong, cannot be expected to teach the Bible, especially where the great majority of the pupils are children of heathen parents. It remains for mission schools to teach this great bulwark of morality and religion. Taking all these things into consideration, it is not strange that most missionaries have accorded to Christian schools an important place as auxiliaries to the preaching of the Word.

As to the place of schools in the scheme of evangelization, there has been no little difference of opinion. In the earlier stages of mission work in China, they were among the chief methods used for reaching the people. Before missionary work was permitted in China itself, schools were begun in what were called the "out-stations" of Singapore, Penang and Malacca. When Hong Kong was ceded to Great Britain in 1842, schools were among the principal means used for reaching the Chinese. The first day-school in Canton was started in 1850. Perhaps in the early days of mission work it was felt that schools were the only means of making an impression on the Chinese. Some have said, "The Apostles opened no schools. Our simple duty is to preach the Word, whether men will hear or whether they forbear." Others say, "Our commission to teach all nations includes the young, who are more impressible, as well as the older, who are hardened by prejudice and sin." Thus, there are missionaries who lay great stress on schools as an evangelizing agency, while there are others who would reject them altogether. Probably there is a just mean, and we must be governed by our surroundings. If it be found impossible to reach the adults ; if they will not listen to preaching, or no converts are gained from those who do listen after years of labor, probably schools should be tried. Wherever we can get the ear of the people, I certainly think that our main dependence should be placed on the oral preaching of the Gospel. Schools, however, are often very good as an entering wedge. When we wish to gain a foothold in a town or village, we can often rent a place as a school-room when no one will rent one as a chapel. An earnest Christian schoolmaster may do a good work in winning men to Christ, in overcoming the opposition and removing the prejudices of the villagers, so that they will be willing to have public preaching. The Chinese all acknowledge that education is a good thing, as they do the healing of the sick, whereas they are suspicious of the public preaching of a new doctrine. Thus schools may be, and often are, the forerunners of other forms of Christian work.

As to the importance of schools for the training

of the children of the Christian converts there is very little difference of opinion. This is a different question from the policy of opening schools as an evangelizing agency. A few missionaries, however, have contended that such schools are not a part of mission work, but should be undertaken entirely by the converts themselves. To send the children of the converted heathen to heathen schools is almost equivalent to relegating them back to heathenism. If a Christian education is important in America, where the common schools are at most non-Christian, much more is it necessary where these schools are anti-Christian.

The question of teaching English in Mission schools is one that has given rise to much discussion. Experience has proved that hitherto such teaching, if not detrimental, has at least been of no direct benefit to mission work. The youth so trained have so many inducements to enter into mercantile and Government positions that almost all have disappointed the hopes of their missionary teachers and have been of no service to the mission. Of course they may have been favorable to Christianity to a certain extent, and occasionally may have contributed to the support of the school which educated them, or to Christian or benevolent objects; but as for directly helping in the work of propagating Christianity they have generally proved failures. Dr. Legge, formerly president of the Anglo-Chinese College in Singapore and Hong Kong, after years of experience, confessed that such teaching failed of its object. He saw around him men in the merchants' offices or in Government employ who had been trained under his care, but only one or two remained for any length of time in mission work. The demand for English-speaking Chinese is so great, their pay, compared with that which Missionary societies can give, is so large, and their position in the Chinese community is so much more pleasant, that unless they really feel the burden of souls resting upon them, they are not likely to devote themselves to the life of self-denial and reproach involved in direct labors for the conversion of their countrymen. In an able paper read before the Shanghai Conference of 1890, Dr. C. W. Mateer, one of the foremost educators in China, contends earnestly in favor of giving all our instruction in the Chinese language and preparing text-books which will become a part of the Chinese literature. He makes the point that an education in Chinese is of special service only as it is thorough ; that a thorough education in his own language is essential to a man's reputation for scholarship amongst his own people, that a training in English leads a man to neglect his own language, that only an education in Chinese will enable a man to use his knowledge effectively, and impart it clearly to his countrymen; that education in Chinese leads a man to live among his own people and exert his influence upon them, and has much less tendency to lift its possessor above the level of his own people than education in English. He says forcibly : " He who is educated in English considers it his chief stock in trade, and expects to live by it. The result is that by a natural necessity he is attracted to a foreign port and finds his place in connection with foreign trade, or in *yamens* having connection with foreign affairs. In such positions his influence for good among his own people generally counts for but little. Moreover, as experience shows, the wreck of his moral character is the common result, and his life counts as so much against, instead of for, the truth. If, on the other hand, he is educated in his own language, he remains amongst his own people. His moral character is conserved. He is looked upon as a man of superior intelligence and attainments. His opinions and his teaching go to break the power of superstition and of prejudice. He is a light in the darkness, and the effect of his life will be for the general uplifting of Chinese society. All this is aside from the special work of preaching the Gospel. If he feels called to this work (as he often does), his education fits him for it in the highest degree,

14

and his reputation, as a man of learning, commands the respect of those who are inclined to look down upon religion with contempt." *

On the other hand there are some who maintain that with a knowledge of English a " wide range of knowledge is thereon open to the student from which he can draw unlimited stores of information." While, with a knowledge of Chinese only, the student is shut up to what he has been taught, if he understand English, the vast store-house of literature, science, history, theology, etc., are thrown open to him. While there is force in the arguments on both sides, the safest conclusion seems to be that English should not be usually taught; but, in exceptional cases, when a man shows a spirit of investigation and the capacity to improve himself indefinitely, it may be well to spend time and money in teaching him English. There is no doubt of the fact that most of the Chinese who study English do so merely with the desire to better their pecuniary position, and as soon as they acquire a smattering sufficient for business purposes leave school for some remunerative employment. A few, however, have used their knowledge of English for the spiritual benefit of their countrymen.

Schools of various grades have been established

* " Records, Shanghai Conference," p. 466.

HAKODATE.

in connection with different missions. The most numerous are the *day schools*. These give primary instruction to the youth in the cities, towns and villages. They are generally intended mainly for the children of the heathen, and no doubt good is done by bringing the truths of Christianity in contact with the impressible minds of childhood. Even more depends on the teacher than on the books taught. The best books, taught by a heathen, or a merely professed Christian teacher, who ridicules the truth of religion and endeavors to exalt Confucius above Christ, are useless. The great need for these primary schools is a truly consecrated Christian teacher. The practice of employing heathen teachers as a makeshift is thoroughly to be deprecated. While the actual daily drill is given by native teachers, the foreign missionaries always examine the pupils on what they have gone over, week by week, and have an opportunity of impressing religious truth on the children and influencing them for good in various ways.

In many missions (as in our own at Canton) most of these day schools are for girls. There are special reasons for this. In the first place the literary education of the girls of China is almost entirely neglected. If they are taught at all, it must be in Christian schools. Then we can reach the men through our chapels and our books, but the women must be reached, either in their homes or by teaching them while young. The great object of these primary girls' schools is to teach them to read the Bible intelligently for themselves. If their hearts are impressed with the truth, as they are married and become mothers, they will teach their children the Christian truths and the Christian hymns they have learned to sing, and the ground will at least be prepared for the full reception of the Divine truth when, in the providence of God, it is brought home to them. All this tends to undermine heathenism and to cause idolatry to relax its hold upon the minds of the Chinese. Though the number of professed conversions may not be numerous, as the heathen parents often refuse to permit their daughters to be baptized, still the influence of religion is not lost. "Educate the mothers of France," said Napoleon, when asked what was the best way to promote the prosperity of the state. By educating the mothers of China in the truths of God's word, we are doing foundation work. The results may be slow in appearing, but they are none the less hopeful. A Chinese who graduated with honor from a foreign college says: "The question of female education in China is of special interest to me. I believe the crying need of China is the elevation of her women and their liberation from the social shackles that bind them. She must remain stagnant so long as she allows her daughters to be made household drudges and denied the right and opportunity to cultivate and cherish an interest in things beyond the four walls of their home. . . . My country-women should have the first claim on the attention, sympathy and charity of Christian people in more favored lands. . . . The seed of a man's faith in the providence of God is planted in his breast by his mother, and no one else can do it half as well. And it is needless to say that the surest way of bringing China into line with America and Europe is by giving to her daughters the advantages of a Christian education." When such enlightened sentiments as these prevail among the Chinese we may rejoice in the hope that China's social regeneration is not far distant. All intelligent thinkers will believe with this Chinese that female Christian education is yet to be among the most powerful reconstructive forces in China.

One of the advantages of day schools is that they are among the most economical forms of Christian effort. In Canton for some $3.00 monthly for rent, and from $3.00 to $5.00 monthly for teacher's salary, we can have a school of 20 to 25 boys or girls under daily Christian instruction. The pupils always furnish their own desks and stationery. The Christian books cost but little and are either furnished by the Mission or paid for by the pupils.

Missions which have an organized school system usually have *Intermediate Schools.* These are generally *Boarding Schools.* They are usually designed especially for the training of the children of the church members, but the most promising pupils from the day schools may be admitted when their parents desire it and are willing to pay the board of their sons or daughters in whole or in part. In the boarding school the pupils are brought much more closely under the instruction and influence of the missionary than in the day school. Their education is carried to a higher degree, and a much better opportunity is afforded the teacher of studying the characters of the pupils and of molding them for good. Their intellectual development too may be better carried on under the daily contact of the foreign missionary. So many advantages have they over the day schools that some would concentrate their efforts on them. But there are also disadvantages. A large and costly building must be provided; the food, and in some cases even the clothing of the scholars, must be given them. This makes the enterprise a much more expensive one. Then the pupils are apt to get accustomed to surroundings and a manner of life which will make their going back to their homes seem a hardship. Apart from their studies, they have little hard work. Their cooking is done for

them ; they do not have to split wood and do household drudgery, nor to work on the farm or at the
bench. These things have to be guarded against
as far as possible. The parents are often required
to pay at least part of the board of their children,
and the pupils to do some work for themselves.
The girls, of course, are taught to do their own
sewing and washing, and to keep their own rooms
in order, and sometimes to help in the kitchen.
Still, the habits of order and punctuality, of neatness and economy which they are taught are a valuable training for life. Then the opportunities of
developing the Christian life and systematic culture
are very great as compared with what they would
have, especially in heathen families. They can have
their prayer meetings and Bible classes, form valuable Christian friendships and render each other
religious help in a way which they cannot do elsewhere. When the scholars go out from such institutions, if the Divine life has really been kindled in
their souls, they cannot but be a power in the community, making itself felt and being a force tending
to reconstruct Chinese society. Though contemned
on account of their fewness in numbers, well-trained,
intelligent Christians have a leavening influence for
good.

There are some *Colleges* and *Seminaries* which
carry literary and religious education to a higher

degree. In Tung Chow, Shanghai, Foochow and elsewhere there are Christian colleges where some of the pupils pay for their tuition. These institutions send out young men well-equipped for life and fitted to take the place of leaders among their countrymen.

The number of Christian schools in the various Missions in China is quite large. The reports for 1889 read at the Shanghai Conference give 16,836 pupils in the Mission schools, 36 per cent. of these were connected with English missions, 58 per cent. with American missions, and .06 per cent. Continental missions. The Methodists have devoted the most attention to schools, having 26 per cent. of the pupils ; then come the Presbyterians with 22 per cent, and the Congregationalists with 19 per cent. None of the rest has 10 per cent. During the five years since the Conference the number of pupils has probably largely increased.

In addition to these Mission schools, there are Chinese Government schools, notably the Tung Wen College of Peking, where Western science is studied, and, like all truth, must tend to shake the confidence of the Chinese in their superstitions, and so far at least prepare the way for reconstruction. Thus Education, and especially Christian Education, is among the forces that are at work in China to break down the old conservatism and prepare the way for something better in the future.

Then let us remember that the young who are receiving this impulse are to take the place of the present generation. They are to be those who will mold the future sentiment of China, and will be the leaders as soon as China is prepared to break with the past and press forward in the path of progress. Several years may elapse before the graduates of these schools make themselves felt, and they will be regarded with jealousy by the literary classes, but the straits in which the country will find itself after the termination of the Japanese war will probably lead them to seek new men and new measures, in the place of those which have signally failed in the time of strain and trial.

CHAPTER XIV.

RECONSTRUCTIVE FORCES.

MEDICAL MISSIONS.

THOUGH all humanitarian work may meet with the Divine approval, the Christian. feels much better satisfied when he has a " Thus saith the Lord," as the secure basis of his action and a Divine command as the great motive to his work. In speaking of Medical missions I wish, therefore, in the first place, to speak of *The Place of Healing in the Divine Plan for the Redemption of the Race.*

In creating man God made him with a soul and a body, and these two have the most intimate relations with one another. Sin in its origin affected, and in its progress still affects, the soul through the body; and body as well as soul suffers from its penalties. In His thoughts of mercy toward our race God pities the body as well as the soul of man. Both were created by God, both have felt the curse of Sin, and both are to share the benefits of God's redemption. As the soul infinitely transcends the body in value and duration, of course this is the chief object of God's solicitude; still, the body is not beneath His notice or His care. In the ministry

KIOTA.—"KUJO MIDZU DERA."

of the Christ on earth, He healed the sick as well as preached the Gospel to men. His tender heart was touched with pity for the lame, the blind, the deaf, the dumb, the palsied, the maimed and the leper. At the grave of Lazarus, while He wept tears of sympathy for the broken-hearted sisters, we are told that he was " indignant in Himself " as He thought of the havoc which death had wrought in the fair form of his friend. He saw Satan's work in men's maimed and decaying bodies as well as in their ruined souls, and " went about," we are told, " doing good, and healing all that were oppressed by the Devil," thus fulfilling his mission to " destroy the works of the Devil."

So, in sending forth His followers, the healing of the body had a place in the thoughts of our Lord as well as the salvation of the soul ; and here let us notice a distinction which is not without significance in showing the place which medical missions should occupy in our scheme for the evangelization of the world. In sending forth the Twelve who were to be His Apostles—those to whom were specially entrusted the continuance of His work and the interests of His Kingdom—He says, " As ye go, preach, saying, The kingdom of heaven is at hand. Heal the sick, raise the dead, cleanse lepers, cast out demons " (Matt. x. 7, 8). Their great work was preaching ; healing was subsidiary. In

Luke x. we have an account of His sending out the Seventy. Here the commission is : "Cure the sick, and say to them, The Kingdom of God is come nigh to you." Notice that the healing of the sick occupies the first place, and the Gospel message is to be announced to them. Here, it seems to me, we have the warrant and the work of the medical missionary—as a physician to heal the suffering body, and as a messenger from God to tell the patient of Jesus. Thus we have two classes of laborers sent out by Christ, ordained preachers who are to preach and found churches, and employ healing as an aid in their great work, and those who are to do the preliminary work of healing, but are never to forget the immortal soul while caring for the perishing body. In the commission given to the Apostles after His resurrection, our Lord seems to have His mind absorbed by the transcendent value of the soul, and says nothing about healing the body. When we turn to the book of Acts, however, we see that the Apostles acted with their first commission still in their minds. Here we find them working on the lines set before them. The first great triumphs of the Gospel under Peter and Paul were accomplished by the preaching of the Word, but in Acts iii. and v. we see how important a place healing occupied in the early spread of Christianity. So Paul mentions " healing," among the gifts of the Spirit (I. Cor. xii. 9). May we not infer from this that the healing of the sick should occupy the first place among the helps to the preaching of the word, as being the only one of these subsidiary agencies mentioned in Scripture? I think this is especially the case in heathen lands. As the Seventy were to do a preliminary work, so now we find medical work of special service in preparing the way for the preaching of the word and the founding of churches among the heathen. In China we find it especially useful in opening new stations, by overcoming the prejudices of the people and showing the benevolent aspect of Christianity in a way that the simplest may understand. We can often rent a house as a dispensary where we find it impossible to secure one as a preaching place. After the people understand our object and hear Christian truth privately, their opposition melts away and they are willing to have public preaching in their midst. Thus medical work proves an entering wedge for the Gospel.

Having spoken of the Divine warrant for medical missions, let us notice the human need. In the Providence of God the concomitant evils of sin and suffering have afflicted our race in every age and in every land. In this same Providence the desire and ability to relieve suffering have accompanied the religion of Jesus. While perhaps one may be justified in saying that, in God's mercy, suffering

15

is less acute among the ruder tribes where the
ability to remove it is small, and that the capacity
to suffer has increased with the nervous tension
which is the result of civilization, and with the
growth of medical skill which is able to relieve it,
still the fact remains that sickness and suffering
are universal.   As a general thing heathen people
have but little ability to remove or alleviate this
suffering.   Even in the more enlightened heathen
lands, as China and India, men have no real knowledge of Anatomy, Physiology, Chemistry or Pathology.   Microscopy, which is so important a factor
in modern physical science is entirely unknown.
The religious views or hoary prejudices of the
heathen prevent any minute investigation of the
true causes of disease.   Their theories are crude
and unscientific and their practice mere em-
piricism.   Thus there is a crying need for medical
missionaries to relieve the ailments of humanity.

As to *sanitation* the Chinese are in utter ignorance.   A physician who has spent over twenty
years in China says: " Their cities and towns are
unspeakably filthy, many of their busy thoroughfares being but elongated cesspools.   Every house-
holder is at liberty to throw any kind of abom-
inable refuse into the public street before his own
door, and sanitary laws, if they exist, are neither
understood nor enforced.   The dwellings of the

poor are minus everything that makes for comfort or conduces to health, and in times of sickness the condition of the sufferers, especially if they have the misfortune to be women, is extremely deplorable." The nasal organs of the Chinese seem to be deficient in sensitiveness, and they endure with apparent impunity stenches that would make a European ill. Many of their rooms are dark and damp. The sewers in the cities are frequently foul, and often, through superstitious notions, are so constructed that the sewage collects in them instead of flowing off. Most of the villages in South China have pools into which all refuse matter is cast. In the winter time these are drained and the rich sediment is used for fertilizing the fields.

Still the Chinese pass much of their time in the open air; the constant use of the fan keeps a supply of fresh air to be inhaled. Then the bright sunshine dries up many impurities, and the heavy rains tend to flush the sewers. So they are fairly healthy, much more so than a foreigner would suppose, who, for the first time, sees their insanitary surroundings.

As to food, they depend chiefly on vegetable diet, which is usually healthful as far as it goes. It is often deficient in quantity and badly cooked. Then they bring on dyspepsia by overloading their stomachs with food at their daily meals, as well as by taking many indigestible substances. However, their simple food and their habit of dieting themselves as soon as they feel unwell preserves most of them in fair, if not vigorous health.

As to clothing they usually show much common sense. Their loose garments do not press upon any vital organ, and allow much freedom of action. The warm wadded garments which they wear in cold weather night and day, while not conducive to cleanliness, preserve them from sudden changes of temperature, and are the best substitute they could have for warm rooms. The heat of the body is thus conserved, and they get their warmth in the most economical way. Their thick, felt-soled shoes keep their feet from the cold ground and form a carpet of the best and most economical kind.

As long as they keep well they do well. But when once they get sick the difference between them and ourselves becomes manifest, much to their disadvantage. Lying on a hard board with nothing but a mat beneath him, often in a dark, foul-smelling room, with no sunlight or fresh air, with none of the neatness and quiet that we associate with the sick-room, the patient is in a miserable plight. With a man it is often bad enough, but with a woman it is usually worse. Her room being in a more retired part of the house will generally be dark and poorly ventilated. She will usually be expected to do more for herself and have less attention. Though the Chinese are almost always careful about the diet of a sick person, according to their notions, these notions are often incorrect.

In the *treatment* of disease the Chinese are far behind the times. There are no regular doctors in our sense of the word; men who have studied the science of medicine and have taken a diploma. Any one may set up as a physician. Many of the doctors are literary men who fail to take a degree in the Literary examinations, and take to medicine by merely reading the native medical books; others are shopkeepers unfortunate in business, or any one else who can get men to take his medicines. The profession is frequently handed down from father to son, often for several generations. In this case many of the remedies are family secrets. There are no medical colleges, nor schools where a systematic study of medicine may be undertaken. The functions of the body are scarcely understood, and the application of remedies is very imperfect.

The Chinese theories of disease and its treatment are very crude. They carry their astrological notions into everything, and medicine among the rest. They fancy there are five elements in nature, metal, water, fire, wood and earth. To these correspond various parts of the body and various diseases. So they divide their remedies into five kinds : hot cold, moist, dry and windy. The Chinese are so confident that this is the truth with regard to the body and its ailments that they will not take any remedy that does not correspond with their notion of the disease. For instance, I once prescribed some sulphur as a laxative, the man refused to take it. He said sulphur belongs to fire; it is one of the elements of gunpowder; I have too much heat in my body already; to take sulphur would add to the heat and make the disease worse. As they have little confidence in their doctors, each man judges of the recipe and will take it or not as suits his own notion of his disease. To be popular and get patients a native practitioner must pander to these preconceived notions of his patient. This want of confidence in their doctors is shown by the custom of calling in several doctors to a case. If the pain or serious symptoms of disease are not removed in a day or so, another doctor is called in, then a third, and so on. Consequently a man is led merely to assuage the pain, or remove some symptom, perhaps quite unimportant, in order to retain the charge of his patient; thus no rational treatment of a serious or chronic case can be attempted. Of course in some cases all that the best physicians can do is to attend to the symptoms as they appear, since the disease must run its course; but in most cases we must seek to remove the source of the ailment.

JAPAN.—CARRYING CHILDREN.

The Chinese physicians take no note of the insanitary surroundings, nor much of the real internal cause of the disease; their only object is to give " cooling " medicine for " hot " diseases, etc., of course their empirical practice is often successful, and some really have some skill in relieving pain and removing disease.

The doctors are frequently to some extent specialists. They divide diseases into " external " or surgical, and " internal " or medical cases. You will frequently see on a doctor's sign, " Both external and internal diseases cured." Many, however, only attempt to extract teeth, or heal ulcers, or treat the eye, or heal skin diseases. In some regards doctors are treated with respect as their employment is considered a benevolent one. But there are so many ignorant quacks and powder and pill mongers that the profession is much looked down upon. They are frequently classed with necromancers and fortune-tellers, and the artful scoundrels who live by their wits and will condescend to any trick to make a penny. Hence Tseng Kwoh Fan or Marquis Tseng, who was an able Chinese statesman and ambassador to Great Britain, exhorts men to put no faith in three things: (1) Buddhism; (2) Tauism; and (3) medicine.

As to the *remedies* for disease, it is strange how an intelligent people, who have had years of experience, should place the confidence they do in many of their remedies. Some are the result of their idolatrous superstitions. Just as they have puppet-shows with music and offerings to the god of fire every autumn to ward off conflagrations during the winter (the dry season), so they organize gaudy idolatrous processions in the spring " hoping to escape the almost annual visitation of the cholera, the germs of which are breeding in the gutters of the streets through which they parade." During the epidemic of the " black plague " in Canton, in 1894, processions with their idols and music paraded the streets day and night. The Chinese frequently let off fire-crackers to drive away the evil demons, which they suppose cause the illness, and, whenever a patient becomes delirious, fancy that an evil spirit is possessing him, and call in the magicians to drive away the demon by their charms and noise and brandishing of swords. Few who live in Christian lands have any idea of the chains in which idolatry holds its victims, even in civilized lands like China. The Chinese doctors " though possessing a considerable amount of empirical knowledge of the properties and uses of certain drugs, are utterly ignorant of their physiological action, and in medicine, as in everything else, the Chinese are enslaved by the traditions of a thousand years ago. To many substances which we know to be either inert, or, at best, of but slight medicinal value, is attributed almost magic power. Ginseng, for instance, a very mild tonic, is firmly believed to have the power of rejuvenating the aged, or restoring the wasted strength of the debauchee, and of working such marvelous changes in the human body that, had our ancient philosophers known of it, they would have given up, as no longer necessary, their search for the " elixir of life." The best qualities of this root are worth more than their weight in gold, and one sees now and then in the *Peking Gazette* an announcement that the Emperor has graciously bestowed a catty of that precious article on some favored minister.

Tigers' bones are given to the weak and debilitated as a strengthening medicine, and those who cannot afford such an expensive luxury may yet obtain some of the strength and courage of that ferocious beast by swallowing a decoction of the hairs of his mustache, which are retailed at the low price of a hundred cash a hair! " * In Canton, when members of the captured rebels were decapitated during the Tai Peng insurrection 1853–5, an American missionary told me that he had seen the Imperial soldiers tear out the gall-bladders of the rebel prisoners just executed and eat them on the spot, thinking that thus they would obtain the

* Dr. A. W. Douthwaite, " Shanghai Conference Report," p. 270.

courage which characterized their enemies, for they suppose that courage resides in the gall-bladder! Thus now in China, as in Europe several centuries ago, the most inert and most disgusting substances are frequently prescribed as remedies for disease. One has but to read the *Pwen Tsao*, the standard Dispensatory of China, to see them.

In surgery the knowledge of the Chinese is almost *nil*. Their superstitious fears and prudish notions prevent them from attempting any real investigation of the dead body. When a European physician applied for the bodies of decapitated criminals to use for dissecting, in order to give some of the native doctors some ideas of anatomy, the official replied that the idea was a good one, but remarked, " There is not a doctor in the city who would dare to cut a dead body, lest the ghost of the deceased should haunt him." The overweening value the Chinese ascribe to astrology has dislocated whatever little practical knowledge of anatomy they may possess. I have seen the charts of a native army doctor, where the wounds are to be treated according to the hour of the day in which they were inflicted, and not according to the parts injured or the instrument making the wound. Acupuncture and the use of the moxa are among the most common remedies of the Chinese.

Female complaints go almost entirely unrelieved,

as prejudice and their ideas of propriety forbid them calling in even their own ignorant male doctors, and they have no female physicians except a few women who deal in what we call "old women's remedies." In childbirth many lives, both of mothers and children, are sacrificed through the ignorance of the midwives. "The profound ignorance of the native faculty, and the seclusion and modesty of the female members of most families open an unlimited field in China for the lady physician, who combines the necessary physical endurance and moral courage with devotion to the self-denying exercise of her profession."

The tendency of heathenism is to dull and harden the heart, and those who suffer from disease receive very little of that *sympathy* which we have learned from our *Master*, and which has become an essential part of our Christian civilization. When God "makes men's hearts soft" through sickness and pain, they are often better prepared to appreciate Christian sympathy and to receive the Gospel message of comfort and hope.

From what has been said it is evident that there is much room in China for Western physicians and surgeons, and it is not strange that Christian hearts have responded to the inarticulate cry for help from the suffering ones in China. Following the example of the Master, and remembering His words,

"Heal the sick," Christian physicians have left their homes in order to aid in the mission work by alleviating pain and curing disease. *Vaccination* was introduced into China by Pearson, a surgeon, in 1805. Before he left China in 1832, he had the pleasure of seeing many of the Chinese securing this protection, and native practitioners conferring its benefits on their countrymen. In 1828 Dr. Colledge, surgeon to the East India Company, opened a hospital in Macao, where he gave special attention to the diseases of the eye. These two physicians were prompted by their own benevolence simply, and were not sent to China specially to treat the Chinese. In 1835 Dr. Peter Parker, who was sent out by the American Board of Commissioners for Foreign Missions, opened an Ophthalmic Hospital in Canton, and thus was the first medical missionary to the Chinese. In 1836 the Medical Missionary Society was founded among the foreign residents in China to aid Dr. Parker in his benevolent work. This society has celebrated its semi-centennial, and its fifty-sixth annual report has been published. In the year 1893 there were 1,608 in-patients in the well-furnished hospital in Canton, and there were 25,542 attendances at the hospital dispensing-room in Canton, and 31,637 at the dispensaries in various parts of the country and city auxiliary to the institution, making a total of nearly 60,000 patients prescribed for during the year. They report that hundreds have given up idol-worship, and scores have been brought to Christ as the result of Christian teaching within its walls. The Chinese have opened two large native hospitals in imitation of the Christian institution, being thus provoked to emulation by the Medical Missionary Society's Hospital. This hospital is now in charge of physicians sent out by the American Presbyterian Board. The English Wesleyans have a flourishing self-supporting hospital in Fat Shan, a large town twelve miles from Canton. The English Presbyterians at Swatow, in the eastern part of the Kwang Tung province, report that of their twenty country stations, seven or eight have had their origin through the patients from their hospitals. "In 1885, out of an attendance of 5,500 patients, over 80 publicly declared their faith in Christ, and earnestly desired to join the church."

The London Missionary Society's physician at Amoy reports that "12,000 to 14,000 towns and villages are yearly represented in the hospital, and that as the result of the cure of one man, seventeen years before, no less than seven Christian congregations had been formed, with a membership of from thirty to one hundred members each." So we might go on with annual attendances of 5,000, 10,-000, 15,000 at the hospitals and dispensaries connected with the various missions in different cities and towns of China. From the island of Formosa Dr. McKay reports that " from the visit of one man to the hospital, there exist four congregations of Christians, with a membership of three hundred and fifty souls, and double that number of adherents, besides flourishing schools." Korea, to which the eyes of the world are now directed, was opened to Protestant missionary effort by means of the labors of medical missionaries.

In 1841 Dr. Parker, while on his way to America, stopped at Edinburgh, and as a result of his visit, a society was organized called the " Edinburgh Association for Sending Medical Aid to Foreign Countries." In 1843 the name was changed to the " Edinburgh Medical Missionary Society." They subsequently opened the well-known " Cowgate Mission Dispensary," which, under the care of Dr. W. Burns Thomson and others, increased in efficiency and influence until similar institutions were opened in Glasgow, Aberdeen, Liverpool, London, Manchester, etc. The society extended its operations in foreign lands until, in 1885, it had one hundred and seventy medical missionaries located in India, China, Africa, Turkey, Syria, Egypt, Rome, etc. Many of the physicians who have come from Great Britain to China have been connected with this noble society.

In the reports of medical missionary work made

JAPAN.—TRELLIS OF WISTARIA, AND NATIVES.

at the Shanghai Conference of 1890, there were sixty-one hospitals, and forty-four dispensaries, with a total attendance in 1889, of 348,439 patients. These institutions are scattered throughout all the provinces of China, occupied by missionary workers.

As to the relative importance of hospitals and dispensaries ; just as the Boarding School is the most efficient means of reaching the young, so the hospital is the most efficient means of reaching the sick. Here all the superiority of Western surgery and medicine may be seen to the best advantage. Cases entirely beyond the reach of native practitioners recover, important surgical operations are performed, and the many modern appliances for relieving disease may be found. The doctor has the patient under his own care for weeks, and permanent relief may be given. Not only so, but the opportunities for religious instruction are much greater. In reply to inquiries by Dr. Dauthwaite, one well-known worker says: "Nearly all admitted to the church in this city have been brought in through the hospital." Another estimates that "one third of the membership is the result of the influence of hospital work." Another says: "The majority of those who have been admitted here to our church were from the hospital." As noticed above, the patients often come from a number of towns and villages for hundreds

16

of miles around, and as they return carry with them the Christian books they have received, and the favorable impressions that have been made on their hearts. Hundreds leave the hospitals with their faith in idolatry shaken and with some seeds of Christian truth in their minds, received under the most favorable auspices. Thus a Christian hospital has a leavening influence in the neighborhood, and not only tends to give favorable impressions of the value of Western medical skill, but also of the Christian benevolence which prompts to its exercise.

Like the Day School in the Educational scheme, the Dispensary has the advantage of spreading the benefits of Christian benevolence over a wide sphere. It is especially valuable in opening new stations, and thus medical missions do the preliminary work for which they are specially adapted. While the dispensary patients are not under the influence of Christianity for so long a time as individuals, the benefits of the institution are extended to a greater number. For instance, as mentioned above, while there were 1,608 in-patients in the Canton hospital there were 25,542 attendance at the dispensary room, while in the branch dispensaries, in various places miles away from the city, there were even a greater number of cases. Thus the wider diffusion of the benefits is secured.

The expense too is much less. An efficient hospital needs large, well-furnished buildings, with a staff of assistants and servants, while a rented room will do for a dispensary, and much good is often done by a medical missionary in itinerations. As in most things, there are advantages in both methods of work, and each has its peculiar advantages. While, as an exhibition of Western skill, the hospital has the decided advantage, as diffusing medical aid to a great number of people at a much lower cost, the dispensary is to be preferred. The one is better suited to pioneer work, while the other is of inestimable value in a permanent mission station. They are of equal value in spreading the knowledge of Christian truth. In both the Gospel is taught at the bedside or publicly, and in both Christian tracts and Scriptures are offered to the patients.

These hospitals and dispensaries are not only institutions for the relief of present suffering, but they are *training schools* where the young men of China receive both theoretical and practical instruction in Western medicine and surgery, and are sent out among their fellow-countrymen, as intelligent and useful practitioners. Thus the benefits of the institution go on to future generations. Especially is this the case in the hospitals, where regular medical classes are formed with a well-arranged curriculum of study. Thus they become medical schools as well as hospitals. Then *medical text-books* have been translated or composed. Drs. Kerr, Hobson, Osgood, Whitney and others have done good work in this direction. These works are valuable acquisitions to the literature of China, and must in the future displace almost entirely the antiquated, irrational, so-called medical works of China. It is to be hoped too that from the young men who go forth from these hospitals, there may arise some who, like Dr. Kitisato of Japan, will add to the general stock of medical knowledge. The Orientals, with their habits of patient investigation and minute and acute observation, have qualities which will, by cultivation, enable them to excel in many respects. We may hope in the future for light to be thrown on Chinese Materia Medica and Pathology by the careful researches of native physicians. If they will only train themselves to do thorough work they will be able to equal the Japanese and even Europeans in accurate observation and skillful practice.

Since Dr. Parker's day a *number* of medical missionaries have come out to China. Dr. J. C. Thomson, in a paper read during the Shanghai Conference of 1890 gives the following statistics: " Our list contains the names of 214 medical missionaries, representing 25 societies ; 100, at this date, are upon the field, though this, with some others, is a constantly changing figure. One hundred are from America. Thirty-eight are ladies; all except two, from America. Of these, five are married.

The pioneer was Rev. Peter Parker, M. D., in 1834. Miss L. S. Combs, M. D., in 1873, was the first female medical missionary to China.

Two natives are on the list, by name, Wong and King, and are probably the first Chinese, male and female, ever to receive foreign medical diplomas.

A number have suffered more or less violence from the natives, as Drs. Lockhart and Osgood; many have retired from ill-health, and others lie buried on the field, as Drs. Wiley, Henderson, Osgood, Schofield and Mackenzie. Dr. Wm. Parker was killed by the fall of himself and horse through a bridge at Ningpo; James, at Hong Kong, and Thomson, at Swatow, were drowned, and Hyslop was massacred by the natives, on the Australian coast. Dr. Kerr has rendered the longest service.

The American Presbyterians send the largest number—34. The American Methodist Mission is next with 31, though the various Presbyterian missions aggregate 66. The London Mission, 20; the American Board, 20; English Presbyterian Mission 18; China Inland Mission, 15; Baptist Mission, 12; American Episcopal Mission, 8; Church Mission, 8.

Most, if not all the provinces, have seen a Medical

missionary, Chili leading with 30; Kwang Tung with 29; Fuhkien 27; Kiangsu 26; Hupeh 11; Chekiang 10; Kiangsi and Formosa, each 5; while Shansi, Nganhwui, Honan, Szchuen, Shensi and Manchuria each have from one to four; still there would seem to be four provinces where there is as yet no established medical mission, viz; Hunan, Kwangsi, Yunnan and Kansuh."

The work of female medical missionaries, though begun later, is of no less importance than that of their brethren. In some respects their work is even more needed as their sex is much more neglected in China than the males. While it is not true, as has been sometimes stated, that the women of China will not consult a foreign male physician, it is undoubtedly true that a fully qualified lady physician has much freer access to her own sex. Dr. Macleish of Amoy says : " The conditions of Chinese social life are such as to render it necessary that a separate institution should be provided for women, where they may receive advice and treatment from an educated physician of their own sex." I doubt, however, if this would be any more advantageous than the plan adopted at Canton where a lady physician is in charge of the female wards in the general hospital.

In addition to the immediate aid rendered to the patients Chinese women are trained as nurses and as medical practitioners by the lady doctors. When we consider how ignorant the Chinese are of any rational nursing and medical treatment of the sick, we see what a wide field is here opened for the benefit of suffering humanity. With Chinese women well qualified as physicians under the instructions of their sisters from the West, and imbued with a true spirit of Christian sympathy, there is a hope for a great improvement in the well-being of the sick in China in the future. Then these women will have opportunities by the bedside of their patients to give Christian instruction and give the consolation of the Gospel to their afflicted country-women. Thus they will be able to counteract the influence of the Buddhist nuns who visit the sick with their simples, and urge upon them greater devotion to the idols, and go to the temples to offer up prayers and offerings in their behalf.

Medical mission work presents to the Chinese the practical, benevolent side of Christianity, which is the most attractive one to them. They are a practical, near-sighted people, and emphasize humanity, while they do not care so much for religion as such. The influence of Buddhism unites with that of Confucianism to make them appreciate the value of kindliness and attention to the wants and sufferings of mankind. Hence it is easy to see how medical missions will tend to uplift China and to be one of the most popular of the Reconstructive Forces which are at work changing the face of Chinese society. Vaccination has become almost universal in South China and has pervaded almost the whole empire. Western treatment of eye diseases is beginning to be known. The young men who complete their course at the hospital schools are in great demand, and readily find employment as doctors at remunerative pay. So great is the demand that the trouble is to keep students long enough to finish a full course of study, and some who obtain a mere smattering are ready to set up as doctors who have studied "Western medicine." Those who go out from the institutions well qualified, especially if, in addition to their knowledge, they have Christian characters will be a power in the community for good.

The foreign medical missionary, if not merely a devotee to his profession as a doctor, but as a missionary he be constrained to enter on this service by sincere love to Christ, will be an influential factor in the work of China's regeneration. He often has intercourse with the high officials, he has men of influence among his patients, and is generally looked up to by the masses of the people. Thus by his personal influence he may accomplish much. Then, as an author, he has influence with literary men, and by his writings he may do much to dispel

CASTLE WALL AND MOAT.

prejudices and to introduce new ideas among those who come within the sphere of his influence.

When we consider the number of hospitals and dispensaries in the different provinces of the empire, the spirit of consecration which characterizes so many of the workers, the physical relief and moral influences that have already gone out from these institutions, and the favorable light in which the medical missionaries are regarded by the Chinese who know of their beneficent work, we may well consider medical missions among the most far-reaching and hopeful of the forces brought to bear upon the ancient empire of China, tending to bring her under the influence of Western progress and of Christian civilization.

CHAPTER XV.

RECONSTRUCTIVE FORCES—CONTINUED.
CHRISTIAN LITERATURE.

FROM of old the Chinese have held literature in great esteem, and pride themselves on China's being "The Land of Literature" (*Men-Meh chi Pang*). In this respect their country has been looked up to as a model by the surrounding nations, and its written language has been, not only the medium of intercourse, but also the standard of literature for the neighboring peoples. For centuries Japan, Korea, Tartary, Thibet and Cochin China had no literature of their own apart from Chinese. The classics and other standard writings of the Chinese have been the study of the scholars among their neighbors. From ancient times China has had a written language, and the art of printing is in all probability a Chinese invention. The people have a superstitious reverence for written or printed paper, and think that they show disrespect to the sages who transmitted the art of writing to them, if they use, for any ordinary purpose, paper which has a Chinese character on it. These feelings tend to

give the printed page a permanence which it does
not have in other lands, and makes the difference
between the spoken word and the written character
all the more marked. Horace's words, "Verba
volat, litera scripta manet," is nowhere more true
than in China.

Seeing that the Chinese hold literature in such
high esteem it is not strange that Christian missionaries have sought to make it a vehicle of conveying
the truths of Divine Revelation to the people.
Though the Roman Catholics, who were first on
the field, have a respectable Christian literature
written in a good style, they have not attempted to
reach the masses of the people as the Protestants
have done, and the issues from their press are not
so numerous. They have made no attempt to give
the Bible in its entirety even to their own people,
and most of their tracts are intended for their converts rather than for the heathen. The three principal forms of Christian literature issued from the
Protestant Mission press of China are the Sacred
Scriptures, and religious tracts, and periodicals.
Many school-books and scientific text-books, written
from a Christian standpoint, have also been prepared and published by the missionaries; also a
number of dictionaries and other helps for learning
the Chinese language. Let us glance at these
forms of Christian literature.

TRACTS AND RELIGIOUS BOOKS.

The Chinese have many moral tracts of their own independently of Christianity. These are usually written by Confucianists, with Buddhistic or Taoistic leanings, and inculcate the virtues most esteemed among the Chinese, as filial piety; and warn against what the writers consider the most prevalent faults and vices of their fellow-countrymen, as infanticide, eating beef, showing disrespect to written paper, etc. Some of these tracts have attained to high repute and are known throughout the Empire, while others have merely a local circulation. Noted among these works are "The Sacred Edict," "Traditions for Reforming Manners," "A Guide to Prosperity," "The Book of Rewards and Punishments," "Light in a Dark Dwelling," "A Precious Mirror for Enlightening the Mind," etc. The first named, written by the Emperor Yung Ching (1746), consists of sixteen rules of conduct, with comments; and it was made the duty of the literati in all parts of the Empire to expound and urge them upon the common people twice a month. This practice, which has largely fallen into disuse, is probably in imitation of the Christian custom of teaching on Sunday. Yung Ching himself was a thorough Confucianist with Buddhist leanings, and was a persecutor of the

Christians. On account of its coming from an Imperial author, as well as being a crystallization of the views of the great body of the literati, this book is held in great repute.

These Chinese tracts are based on the innate knowledge of right and wrong that is confined to no one land; but the motives appealed to are usually superstitious and frivolous. They attempt to deceive, coax or frighten men for their good, and deal with the common people too much as some thoughtless parents do with their children. Speaking of these books, Dr. J. L. Nevins says: " They are a pitiable commingling of light and darkness, truth and error, the inconsistency and incongruity of which the people seem utterly unable to perceive." They present a fair picture of the moral and religious views of the Chinese. Their ideas of rewards and punishments are a mixture of Confucian notions of reward for virtue in this life and a good name among posterity, and Buddhist ideas of punishments and rewards in the future. They have lists of merits and demerits, arranged like a debit and credit account. The Buddhist notions of the emptiness of earthly things are also quite common. The idea of a Divine revelation is not contrary to Chinese opinions, and many of these books profess to be revelations from some one of the gods, who has manifested himself to the writer and com-

17

manded him to make the message known to others.

These books are distributed gratuitously, especially to the students at the Government examinations. The motive is a selfish one, as the man who bears the expense of publishing and distributing them acquires a fund of merit; the consciousness that he is trying to do good may also be a motive with some.

In this connection may be mentioned the anti-Christian tracts, of which there are not a few. These are often exceedingly scurrilous, obscene and blasphemous. They are sometimes illustrated by rude cartoons of our Lord Jesus as a hog nailed on the cross, and lewd pictures representing the Christians as immoral. They are so bad that they must defeat their own object with all thinking people who see they must have come from a bad source, but they often accomplish the purpose of those who get them out by stirring up the minds of the mob against Christianity. One of these, called " A Death-Blow to Corrupt Doctrine," has attained an unenviable notoriety as a means of instigating mobs. Though these publications were originally directed against the Roman Catholics, they make no distinctions, but have the same political object of opposing all " foreign religions."

Christian missionaries have endeavored to supplant this bad or worthless literature by the good.

Hence tracts, inculcating Christian truths and teaching morality from a Christian standpoint, have been printed in great numbers in all parts of China. Peking, Hankow, Shanghai, Ningpo, Foochow and Canton, and Hong Kong, have been the points from which most of these have been issued ; and the Tract Societies of Great Britain and America, as well as local societies and different missions, have been active in the production and circulation of these books. In size they vary from thick volumes to sheet tracts. Some of them have been ephemeral, or have had merely a local circulation, while others have become a part of the permanent Christian literature of China, and are issued in different forms and dialects and localities. Some belong to Apologetic literature, while most are didactic and hortatory. They vary in style from the antique, classic style, specially suited to scholars, to the simplest colloquial, intended for women and children.

These tracts, distributed at the market towns and the examination halls, in the shops and by the wayside, will reach many a nook and corner unreached by the voice of the living preacher ; by the novelty of the truths they teach and the earnestness with which these truths are presented they will excite ripples of thought in the still and stagnant pools of village mental life. They excite questions in the minds even of the most sluggish, and prepare the way for the living preachers of the Word. Thus they are a leaven to change the monotonous current of thought into new channels, and will prove of no little value among the Reconstructive Forces at work in China. When we consider their great numbers, millions of pages annually, the adaptability to the masses of the people, and the fundamental truths that they teach, we may begin to realize something of the important part these little messengers of truth are having in the great work of China's redemption.

SCRIPTURES.

The translation and distribution of the Sacred Scriptures has always been one of the most important parts of the work of Protestant missions. The introduction of the Bible into China is not a new thing. The Nestorians, in A. D. 635, brought the Syriac version of the "True Scriptures, the Sacred Books," into China, and the celebrated Nestorian tablet, erected in 781, speaks of the "twenty-seven sacred books" as having been translated into Chinese. This refers, of course, to the New Testament. In A. D. 1200, John de Monte Corvino, a Franciscan monk, was sent by Pope Nicolas II. as a representative at the Mongol court. He is said to have translated the Psalms and the Gospels into Chinese.

NAGASAKI.

The Jesuit missionaries, three hundred years ago, translated portions and perhaps the whole of the New Testament, but seem to have taken no pains to circulate them. A Chinese version of the New Testament in seven volumes is found in the Vatican library, and another manuscript version is in the British Museum, and was studied by Robert Morrison before he came to China. Bible translation and circulation has been an important factor in the modern missionary movement of the present century. The first whole Bible, including both testaments, was published at Serampore, India, in 1820; the translation was the joint work of Dr. J. Marshman, the well-known colleague of Wm. Carey, and Joannes Lassar, an Armenian who had lived at Macao, China, and was a teacher at the Calcutta Government College. Two years later, in 1822, Morrison and Milne's version was published at Malacca. These were imperfect and preliminary, and served rather to pave the way for subsequent versions than to be of much actual service for distribution. After missionaries had gained a foothold in China itself, as a result of the treaty of Nanking, signed August 29, 1842, they began to plan for an acceptable version of the Bible. The Delegates' version of the New Testament was finished in 1850. This was a decided advance, and is still largely circulated. On the Old Testament, the English and American translators divided, and the work of the English scholars appeared in 1853, while that of the Americans, in a simpler style, was not published until 1862. In 1853, also, Goddard's version of the New Testament appeared. This is an admirable version, and as revised by Dr. Lord, of the same mission, is now used by the Baptists in China. A version of the New Testament has also been made by M. Goury of Peking, for the use of the Greek Church in that city. In 1890, a large body of Protestant missionaries met at Shanghai, and arranged for a Union version of the whole Bible, to be made in three styles : the higher classical style, which is most acceptable to the scholars, a simpler style more useful for the masses of the people, and a version in the mandarin colloquial, which is the spoken language of Northern and Central China. In addition to this, Rev. G. John, of Hankow, has translated the New Testament and some portions of the Old in a very acceptable form, which is having a large circulation, especially in Western China. While a uniform version of the Bible is, in many respects, desirable, the great thing is that the Chinese become acquainted with the momentous truths of God's revealed Word, and this may be accomplished, in His providence, in one way as well as another.

The work of distributing the Scriptures is actively

carried on in all parts of China. In 1889 the three great Bible societies at work in China—the British and Foreign, the American, and the Scottish— reported 21 foreign agents, 213 colporteurs, and a circulation of 454 Bibles, 22,402 New Testaments, 642,131 Scripture portions, i. e. single gospels, etc. Total 665,987.

When we remember that the entrance of God's words into the mind gives light, we must feel that over half a million copies of portions of God's revealed truth, annually reaching the Chinese, must be a power for good. Then, too, when we recollect that these are almost altogether *purchased* and not simply accepted by the recipients, we feel that there is hope that much of the seed has fallen into good ground, and may confidently expect that it will bring forth fruit to the glory of God. Even though much of the seed should be wasted, enough will germinate to make this form of Christian effort among the most efficient forces in the regeneration of China. There is a dynamic force in a new idea, and especially when this new idea is a truth fresh from the Word of God. The unseen forces, working in the minds of men, are often more powerful than visible ones, working from without.

Besides giving the Bible to the people of China in the usual written language, it has been provided for them in various colloquial dialects. The Scriptures have been translated, in whole or in part, into nine main colloquial dialects of China. In five of these, the Chinese characters have been used to express the spoken language, in two, versions have been printed both in characters and in Roman letters, and in two the versions are printed in Roman letters only. There are advocates of representing the local dialects of the Chinese in both of these forms. Some local dialects lend themselves more easily to one method and others to the other. Whatever means may be used, the one object of the translators has been to bring the precious truths of Divine revelation into contact with the minds, and within the comprehension of the understandings of the lowest of the people. Thus the effort has been made to reach the lower strata of Chinese society as well as the higher, the unlearned as well as the learned, those whose minds are reached through the ear, by hearing the Word read, as well as those who are reached through reading it with their own eyes. With the blessing of God's Spirit on this truth, we may hope for a movement among the dry bones, and the quickening of the dull minds of the ignorant masses of China. We may look forward to the times when these men and women, looked down upon by the native literati in their superciliousness, may be won for Christ.

PERIODICAL LITERATURE.

Let us now glance at *Periodical Literature* as one of the factors in China's elevation. Periodical literature is not unknown in China; the *Peking Gazette* has been issued for 1,000 years, and has a daily circulation of some 10,000 copies. But this is a Court Circular or a Government Record, rather than a newspaper in our acceptation of the term. Unless this be an exception, the missionaries were the first to publish periodicals in China. Previous to 1860 there had been eight religious and no secular periodicals published. Of the 76 on the list prepared by Dr. Farnham for the Shanghai Conference in 1890, 40 were religious and 36 secular. There were 35 monthlies, 8 weeklies and 20 dailies, 1 semi-monthly and 2 occasional. Of the 31 still published in 1890, 15 were religious and 16 secular. Most of the Chinese secular newspapers were started and maintained by foreign capital, and they were frequently issued from the office of an English newspaper, but under the editorial care of a native editor. These papers are usually mildly pro-foreign, but they generally follow the wishes and opinions of the native officials within whose jurisdiction they are published; to oppose them in any way would lead to suppression. Hence there are no opposition journals, and the papers cannot be looked upon as

the organs of public opinion. They have to be exceedingly careful not to incur the dislike of the
officials in any way.

The religious periodical press has proved an important aid in spreading a knowledge of the truth.
The secular news, as well as that from the churches,
is eagerly sought for by many besides the Christian
converts. Chinese in the Straits Settlements and
America are glad to get items of intelligence from
their native land. Some of these publications circulate among the better class of officials, and their
impressions with regard to Christianity are doubtless
molded, to some extent, at least, by getting an inside view of affairs from a Christian standpoint.
To the native Christians these papers and magazines
form a bond of union, and a field where the leaders
among them may publish their views of truth and
of current events. Then they tend to beget a taste
for reading among our young people. Of course
news of the progress and trials of the Cause, and
the discussion of matters of present-day interest,
will attract more readers than ordinary tracts will.
Thus the Christian periodical press of China has a
place peculiarly its own, and is a factor which must
be taken into consideration when we think of the
forces which are at work in China tending to reform
and reconstruction. Thus it is an important part

of the Christian machinery by which we are endeavoring to uplift China.

SCHOOL AND TEXT BOOK SERIES.

The *School and Text Book Series* of publications, organized at the first Shanghai Missionary Conference in 1877, is also a lever to lift off the heavy mass of conservatism which is weighing down the minds of the young in China. The Chinese are beginning to feel a desire for Western science, and, as has been remarked above, it is highly important that it should come to them, especially to the children of Christian parents, without the stamp of infidelity and of agnosticism impressed upon it in passing through the hands of some Western scientists who pride themselves on their opposition to a Divine revelation. We who claim that nature as well as the Bible is a revelation of the Creator, do not want the youth of China to drink in anti-Christian sentiments with their first draughts of scientific knowledge. Schools of Western science have already been established in China under heathen auspices, where science is taught in the narrowest acceptation of the term. The late Dr. Alex. Williamson, in a paper read at the Conference of 1890, shortly before his death, says forcefully: " We desire books pervaded by a Christian tone, true science and science up to date when the books are on scientific subjects—but science not ignoring the ineffable Author of all, or hiding from view His glorious attributes, which, the more one knows, the profounder he bows before Him in wonder and adoration, and seeks to commend his own little life to His acceptance and service."

I look upon the present action of the Chinese Government in this respect as being simply suicidal. They are establishing schools and colleges in which science, pure and simple in its narrowest acceptation, is taught to the exclusion of both mental and moral science. Science alone is allowed in their translations, and they believe that science in this sense will strengthen and advance the nation. They make a great mistake.

The students enter these schools with their respect for Confucius and the morality which he inculcated, and come out believing neither in God nor demon, sage nor ancestor. " This sham science, divorced from its author, will be the ruin of their country. It destroys a belief in a personal God, the soul, a hereafter, and leads to the denial of many moral and social duties to which they at present hold fast. Moreover, it undermines the very basis and framework on which their government stands. True religion in conjunction with science alone can save the nation. . . . From the very commencement of

RAIN COATS.

their history the Chinese have invariably placed the moral aspects first."

This committee had published during the 13 years of its existence up to 1890, 84 books beside 40 wall charts of various subjects, and had issued about 30,000 copies of these works. The net average from sales was about $700 per annum. The first name on the list of Chinese subscribers was that of the late Marquis Tseng, who gave $30. " Many other influential Chinese officials and gentry subscribed." Since then this committee has published many more works on Mathematics, Physics, Natural History, History, Geography, Physiology, Biology, etc. These publications will do much to extend the area of Chinese knowledge, hitherto so contracted, and to break down prejudices. They will no doubt rank high among the agencies employed, in the Providence of God, in breaking up the ice under which the mind of China has been imprisoned so long.

Chinese literature represents 3,000 years of mental activity, and ours 1,800 years of Christian development. They have come into contact during the last thirty years, and while we may derive some good from the East, China must feel the results of the impact with the West in the correction of many defects, the quickening of sluggish thought, and the impartation of knowledge more valuable than that of her sages,—the knowledge of salvation.

18

Besides these tracts, Scriptures and school-books, many other books have been translated or written for the use of the Chinese. Commentaries and notes on the Scriptures have been issued in great number; devotional works and Christian biographies, treatises on theology and experimental religion, catechisms and hymn-books have presented the best thought of Western minds on the most important topics that can claim human attention. Bible dictionaries and Bible text-books have been compiled to aid the Chinese native Christians in understanding the Word of God. Works on homiletics and elocution to teach the native preachers how best to reach their audiences and to expound the Bible, have been prepared. Thus, through the labors of the missionaries in their studies, the literature of China has become enriched by new truths, valuable thoughts, useful suggestions, and fresh vehicles for the feelings of devotion. Books for the young have been published, written in the simplest style and illustrated with attractive pictures. Controversial works have been composed, contending against current errors of doctrine and faults of life. Thus a great body of literature has been found, and the writings of the Protestant missionaries of China already amount to thousands of volumes.

CHAPTER XVI.

CONTINUED CHRISTIAN MISSIONS.

RECONSTRUCTIVE FORCES.

But the most powerful factor in China's regeneration remains to be mentioned—the preaching of the Gospel. If the work of the pen is more permanent, that of the human voice, bearing testimony to the most momentous truths, from a full heart, filled with love for man and a desire to glorify God, is still more effective. This is God's own chosen means of spreading the truth. " As 'ye go, *preach*," says the Master. " Go ye into all the world, and *preach the Gospel* to every creature " is the missionary's commission. If this is put among the forces which reach China from the West, it is not because it is of the West. The preaching of the Gospel is from heaven, like the truth which is proclaimed. We are told that it is " the power of God for salvation to every one which believeth." It is for the world, and commends itself to every man's conscience in the world. It is accompanied by the Divine power of the Holy Spirit whenever proclaimed in faith in Him. The preaching of the Word has wrought marvelous changes in the West, and is, no doubt, yet to accomplish wonderful things in the East. The truth has a power in itself to influence men's minds, and when its proclamation is attended by the power of the Spirit to touch men's hearts and mold their wills, it is irresistible. When Robert Morrison came to China in 1807, the captain of the ship said to him: " Do you really expect, Mr. Morrison, to convert the Chinese ? " "No, I do not," was his reply, " but I expect that God will do it." What this pioneer missionary said is the language of every true missionary to-day. Our trust is in God, and in His own appointed means for the propagation of His Truth—the public oral proclamation of the Word.

While this is the great lever to overturn old superstitions and introduce new truth, both by awakening the heathen and building up the native Christians, still it is not the only means of making disciples of the nations. In the earlier stages of mission work in China public preaching was out of the question. Dr. Morrison, during his life of twenty-seven years in China, probably never attempted it. What Christian instruction he gave to those who were influenced by him was given in secret, behind closed doors. His work was almost exclusively literary. Dr. Milne, who joined him seven years later, had to leave Macao on account of the opposition of the Portuguese Roman Catholics, and finally settled in the Straits Settlements, where he did efficient service and wrote a tract, " The Two Friends," which has perpetuated his influence in all parts of China. He also, with Dr. Morrison, began the first Christian Chinese periodical in 1815, called the Chinese Monthly Magazine. It was only after China was opened by the treaty of 1842 and Hong Kong was made a British colony, that preaching could be used to any extent.

There is still some difference of view among missionaries as to the practical value of street preaching as a means of bringing men to Christ. Papers taking opposite views were read before the Shanghai Conference. One claims that the throngs which attend public preaching are only "an evanescent phase of mission life," and that "public preaching in China has not been followed by such results as were at first hoped for." Another writer holds that "among the direct agencies of missionary work this must ever hold the pre-eminence. It is the Divinely appointed means of publishing abroad the " Glorious Gospel of the Blessed God." Another, that the preaching of the Gospel to the heathen " should be esteemed the most precious privilege of the missionary," and that we may rest assured that it will be " the chief means of China's redemption." Perhaps the experience of men has been different in different parts of China, and this accounts for the difference of view. For myself, I believe that this is the Divine plan and should be emphasized, yet that public preaching does not exhaust the meaning of the commission to " teach " or " disciple " the nations. Paul spoke both publicly and from house to house. Our Lord used private conversation as well as public discourse to lead men to a knowledge of the truth. All means should be used " so we may win some " to Christ. A sanctified common sense is a good guide ; and yet we should never forget that the proclamation of the Gospel as a herald is the main means contemplated in the Divine plan. This should be subordinated to nothing else. God's blessing has rested upon it in other lands and will rest upon it in China. It is the means of diffusing abroad the knowledge of the truth, and by its means China is gradually becoming more and more like " Christian " lands, where men have some acquaintance with the Bible, and know their duty to God. Of course much private instruction and conversation is usually needed before the hearers will become converts. The preaching of the Word must ever be one of the great means of leavening the masses of China with Divine truth. Most missionaries devote most of their energies to this pioneer work. " The evangelization of the

heathen " is the sole object of some missionary
societies. Thus preaching is, and probably ever
will be, the chief means of the religious reconstruction of the masses of the Chinese people. It is not
practiced to any extent by the Roman Catholics, but
is characteristic of the open methods of Protestant-
ism.

The *growth* of mission work in China has been
most encouraging. The earliest English missionaries were followed by others, and in 1829 Messrs.
Bridgman and Abeel came to China as the first representatives of the American churches. Others,
among whom was Dr. S. Wells Williams, followed
in the thirties, but it was after the opening of the five
ports and the cession of Hong Kong in 1842 that
modern Protestant mission work may be said to have
begun. The great empire of China, so long closed,
was now opened in answer to the prayers of God's
people, and they began to realize that they must do
their part of the work, and send forth men to enter
the newly opened doors. After the Anglo-French
war of 1856–61 and the treaty of Tientsin in 1861,
a new era began. More ports were opened to foreign trade, and China was, for the first time, really
opened to the preaching of the Gospel, for missionaries were granted the right to travel throughout
the empire and preach. The growth of mission
work in China has been steady, if not rapid.

In 1842 there were   6 communicants.
" 1853 " " 350 "
" 1865 " " 2,000 "
" 1876 " " 13,035 "
" 1886 " " 28,000 "
" 1889 " " 37,287 "

There are now (1895) about 50,000 communicants in the various Protestant churches of China.

Since I arrived, in 1856, I have seen an increase in the number of communicants of some one hundred and twenty fold. The Hong Kong Register gave the Roman Catholic statistics for 1889 as follows :

Bishops	41	Colleges	34
European priests	664	Convents	34
Native "	559	Native converts	1,092,818

The statistics of Protestant mission work for 1889 are as follows :

Missionaries 598
Missionaries' wives 390
Single women 316
                                  Total 1,304

Communicants 37,288
Pupils in schools 17,000
Native preachers, ordained 209
Native preachers, unordained and teachers 1,210
Bible women 180

SHINTO PRIEST.

Of these missionaries, 724 were British, 513 American, and 59 Continental (German) ; of the ordained native preachers, 53 were laboring in connection with British, and 147 in connection with American Missions. Of the 522 organized Chinese churches, 94 were entirely self-supporting, and 49 other partially so. Of the pupils in Mission Schools, 6,079 were in those of the British Missions, 9,757 in those of the American Missions, and 1,000 in those of the Continental Missions. The contributions from the native churches amounted to $36,884.51, or about $1.00 per member.

The growth of the native churches is one of the most hopeful signs of mission work. Christianity can never spread rapidly in China as long as it is looked upon as something belonging to foreigners. As it becomes indigenous, and the heathen Chinese see its fruits in the renewed lives of their neighbors, and hear its truths proclaimed from the lips of thoroughly renewed and wholly consecrated men among their own countrymen, it will become more and more a power in the land. Each little company of regenerated believers will be a nucleus around which other renewed souls will gather, and each little church will be a light-bearer amid the surrounding darkness of heathenism. When woes overtake the land, these little companies of believers can point their neighbors to God, the only source of consolation; when instruction is needed, they can point to that true wisdom which is found in God's Word alone. These churches will be the connecting link between the Christianity of the West and the masses of China—conducting wires along which the power and light and warmth of the Spirit will flow into the coldness and darkness and immobility of heathenism. It is to these Christian bodies, scattered throughout the provinces of the empire, that we are to look for the recuperative power which is to change society in their native land.

The advance of Christian missions in China has been like that of an army—*a struggle*. The mere fact of the removal of legal barriers to the spread of Christianity, though not an unimportant factor, has has been one of the smallest factors in the problem. The religion of Christ cannot make any true progress through force or strategy. Its conquests are the triumphs of truth, patience and love. "The weapons of our warfare are not carnal, but mighty through God." We must win the hearts of the people, not through flattery or cajolery, but "by the manifestation of the truth to every man's conscience in the sight of God." All that we want is access to the people. The preaching of the Gospel, though accorded by treaty, has been opposed openly or secretly by most of those in authority in China. With the duplicity which is so characteristic of them, the mandarins frequently grant requests and put out proclamations to carry out the provisions of treaties, while they secretly scheme to defeat these rights. The literati, who have great influence with the people, though sometimes personally well-disposed, rarely have the courage to stand up for foreigners or for the Chinese identified with them. Especially has every attempt to gain a foothold in the country been opposed by those in positions of authority and influence. The treaties, as originally published and understood, gave missionaries the right of residence in the interior, and also to rent, buy and build houses, etc. In 1871 China endeavored to add conditions which virtually nullified the former privileges. Since then they have tried in every way to prevent our extending the area of Christianity, particularly by residence or building. Especially has this feeling of hostility been prevalent since the trouble with France in 1884. The Chinese fancied that a first-class European power was afraid of them, and they began a policy of restricting the foreigners in every way. This war with Japan may lead them to see their mistake.

In 1884 a persecution of Christianity was started in Kwang Tung (Canton), by the Imperial High Commissioner, Pang Yu Lin. He was an able and popular official, but well known for his anti-foreign and anti-Christian proclivities. On his arrival in Canton the heathen party at once circulated reports that Christianity was to be suppressed. He issued a rabid proclamation in which he said that China would not hold herself responsible for any foreign building destroyed by popular violence. This was construed into a permission to the mob to tear down chapels and foreign residences. In the course of a few weeks no less than eighteen Protestant chapels were torn down or robbed. Many of the native Christians were beaten and otherwise maltreated. In Canton city the chapels were threatened and only preserved from destruction by the activity of the Consuls. In the proclamations the native Christians were spoken of as rebels, and urged to repent. After this violent outbreak caused by the French war, things settled down, but the secret policy is still to restrain the foreigner. More recently a similar outbreak has occurred in the Yang Tsze valley, encouraged by Chang Chi Tung who was the Viceroy of Kwang Tung at the time of the riots there. Chapels, both Roman Catholic and Protestant, were attacked; two Englishmen were killed, and many riots occurred. Later still, in the jurisdiction of the same astute, cunning, implacable viceroy, the massacre of Sung Po has occurred, where two Swedish missionaries were murdered, and all who helped them were punished, while the officials who planned and the ruffians who committed the murder have gone free. Even in 1894 the Christians in Kwang Si Province have been persecuted. In one place they have been boycotted and prevented from building themselves a little meeting-house. In another place, Wu Chau city, we have been driven out for the third time. " The chief mandarin who should have helped and protected us, instead stirred up the people, had false placards put out, sent soldiers and a number of roughs to stone our chapel and drive away our preacher."

Thus Christianity has had to make its way in spite of all kinds of opposition. Yet all this, trying as it is, will advance its final triumph. The native Christians are purified by passing through the fire ; insincere and faint-hearted men are prevented from joining themselves with us ; and, as after the murder of Rev. J. A. Wylie last year, in Moukden, imperial edicts have granted fresh protection to Christianity. God watches over His own cause and causes even " the wrath of man to praise Him." The conduct of the christians under unjust and cruel persecutions, and their forgiving spirit and patience under injury, may do more for the cause than much apparent success may accomplish.

The *character* of the native converts has generally shone out brightly during persecution. Very few have dishonored their profession, and some have been noble confessors. The first Protestant martyr in China, an old man named Chea, refused repeatedly to recant, and was drowned by his neighbors for being a Christian. Many have been excluded from the clan, boycotted and beaten. During the war of 1884, several Tartar soldiers stepped forth from the ranks and acknowledged themselves Christians, and were imprisoned by an intolerant commander. Only last year (1894), "Two colporteurs were cruelly beaten and had their clothes and money taken away from them. Two others were robbed and stripped of their clothing, had their hands tied behind their backs, and were left on the road. One of them, with his teeth, untied the other, and they begged clothing at a village which they entered after dark." The Chinese Christians have not been deterred from their profession and service for Christ by these trials. These things encourage us to hope much from the stability of our Chinese converts.

As to liberality, they have shown a commendable spirit of self-reliance and manliness. Each contributes, on an average, about $1.00 a year for Christian work. This is probably about 3 per cent. of the average monthly income. Some are quite liberal, and in our mission it has not been unusual for men to give a month's income in cases of special contributions. Some wealthy Chinese, as Mr. Ah Hop of Foochow, have given large sums for the prosecution of missionary work among their fellow-countrymen.

While missionaries, like pastors at home, often have to grieve over the faults and failings, and occasionally over the defection of their converts, yet, according to my experience, they do not compare unfavorably with professed Christians at home. When we consider the force of hereditary influences and of daily environment, they are more steadfast than we might expect; while many of them might be examples to those in more favored lands by their faithfulness in confessing Christ and earnestness in urging the claims of the truth on their neighbors. Some of the native preachers are able expounders of the Word of God and active, earnest leaders in the churches. By their prayerfulness, their devotion to their work and their spirit of consecration, some of our Chinese preachers stand well. These leaders will make their mark on Chinese society and prove valuable forces in the onward movement of China in the line of true progress.

As to the *social status* of the Chinese converts : while it is still true, as in apostolic days, that " not many wise men after the flesh, not many mighty, not many noble, are called," yet the Christian converts are not from the dregs of the people, as their proud heathen countrymen sometimes pretend. They are mainly from the middle classes. The

19

more thoughtful among the shopkeepers, the physicians, the farmers and the laborers, as well as the more intelligent among the women, are attracted to Christianity. It is true our converts are from among the more religiously inclined of the common people, rather than from among the atheistic literati, and hence are often looked down upon by that supercilious class. But some of the literati have become Christians, and many of the Christians have well-trained minds, and are men who can hold their own in any discussion with any one.

As to the *methods* in which this Christian work is carried on, they are chiefly preaching in chapels and by the wayside during itinerating tours. These vary in different parts of the field in some details, but are substantially the same. We have our chapels on the most frequented thoroughfares, and invite the passers-by in to hear the Gospel preached ; often the service is begun by singing a hymn, or by conversing with a few hearers, until a crowd gathers. Then a text is taken, or a passage from the Bible read, while we expound and enforce the truth taught. The people come and go as they can spare the time or feel interested in the preaching. We generally have several speakers who spend about half an hour each in preaching. Meanwhile an opportunity is offered to all who wish to inquire about or discuss the truths heard, either in an after-meet-

GOLD SACHIHOKO.

ing or in a side-room where Christian books are on sale. In tours in the country we are accustomed to visit the market-towns on market-days, or to call at the shops on other days. On market-days we soon have a crowd in an open space or under a tree by the wayside, and among them we find some interested hearers and men ready to purchase Christian books at a small price. Or we preach from the boat to the crowds gathered on shore, and endeavor to point out the road to eternal life. Then we try to engage in conversation with the guests at the tea houses' by the roadside, or those whom we meet on the way. Thus in one way and another, we endeavor to cast in the good seed of the Word, assured that God's Word will not return unto Him void, but will accomplish that whereunto it has been sent.

As to the *prospects of success* they are encouraging. When Judson was asked what the prospects of success in Burma were, he said, "Just as bright as the promises of God." Even some Christians seem to have no very clear views of what these promises are. No doubt they include the offer of the Gospel to all, but do they mean that every heathen man will be converted? By no means. At the last day many will be found at Christ's left hand. We are taught by our Saviour Himself that "Wide is the gate and broad the way that leadeth to destruction, and many there be which go in thereat, and that there are but few who find the narrow way," and enter the " straight gate." Just as of old God selected the Jews from among the nations of the earth to be a witnessing nation, so now we read that God hath visited the Gentiles " to take out of them a people for His name," to be a witnessing people. So Paul says: " I endure all things for the elect's sake, that they may also obtain the salvation which is in Christ Jesus, with eternal glory." So the object of the present dispensation is, to make manifest God's elect among all the nations of the earth, and the duty of the Christian missionary is to make the offer of a full, free salvation to every man. Hence all calculations as to heathenism gaining on Christianity by natural increase in the population, even if true, are beside the question. God converts men as individuals, and not as nations. The individual is the New Testament unit of society. " The ax is laid at the root of the trees, *every tree* that bringeth not forth good fruit is hewn down, and cast into the fire." Hence the offer of salvation must be made to men as individuals, and God uses converted men as the salt of the earth and the light of the world. The work of the missionary is to bring the magnet of the truth into close proximity to the particles of earth. The true iron feels the attraction and moves

toward its source. "My sheep hear My voice."
"He that is of the truth," responds to the force of
the truth. While we look forward with joy to "the
new heavens and new earth wherein dwelleth righteousness," our present duty is lovingly and earnestly
to urge the claims of the Christ on every man,
knowing that our Master's promise is that some will
be saved. Success is not to consist in the conversion of the mass, much as we long for such a consummation, but in the manifestation of God's
chosen ones—those who love light rather than
darkness.

The ruling missionary motive is the glory of
the Son of God, and not benevolence merely, however great a force this may have as the secondary
motive. The king made the marriage feast "for
His son," however great His grace in inviting the
guests (Matt. xxii). The success of missions consists in the glory accruing to Jesus. This, and not
the numbers, or the social station, or the political
importance of the converts is the test of success.

Then there is a success that does not appear in
missionary reports. The *untabulated results* of
the preaching of redemption are greater than those
which can be put on paper. The truth is a force,
and when this is Divine truth fresh from heaven,
it has a dynamic power. We cannot measure the
force of the electricity in the earth by counting the

number of trees or houses struck by lightning. Just as little can we estimate the power of the preaching of Christ by the number of baptisms. Prejudices are removed, suspicions dissipated, men's confidence in their idols shaken, the power of superstitions broken, and much preparatory work done. All these things tell on the final result.

Nor is *time* an essential element in the Divine working. The human part of growing a crop on the earth often involves much more time than the Divine part. Cutting down the forests, removing the stones, plowing the soil and casting in the seed consume more time than the germination of the seed. So the preliminary work in missions may be longer than the actual work of ingathering. Men sometimes apologize for the comparative slow growth of conversion in some places, as though it were merely an educational work. While it is true that the crop will usually be proportioned to the preceding labor, yet the Divine side preponderates in Christian work, and God usually works in crises. He " cuts short His work in righteousness." His judgments often come after impending a long time—a forty days' flood after one hundred and twenty years of warning ; so with His blessings. Faith looks to God and is never disappointed, while calculation is of the earth, and speaks from the earth. Success depends more on God than on man ; on prayer, than on effort. Yet success of mission work in China has been encouraging in the past, and by God's blessing, will be far more encouraging in the future.

In speaking of the future success in mission work in China, let it be remembered that, under God, this must depend mainly upon the native churches. Foreigners have planted Christianity in China, and their wisdom and experience and higher type of piety will probably long be needed to advise and guide and incite the native Christians. But, after all, the main work in the evangelization of a people must be done by that people themselves. It is well known that the Japanese are noted among Asiatic converts for their efforts at self-support and self-government as Christians. Have the Chinese the qualities which give us reason to hope that they will take up the work of the propagation of religion among themselves? May we safely commit the sacred deposit of the truth to their safe-keeping in the future? I think we may. While not so impetuous and so self-reliant, perhaps, as the Japanese, on the other hand, their very conservatism will tend to keep them in the "mold of doctrine" wherein they have been cast, and make them hold fast the "form of sound words," without running after every theological novelty that comes up. When entrusted with self-government, though occasionally making mistakes, as was natural, they have usually justified the confidence placed in them. Their efforts for self-support and self-help, too, have been successful. There are now over one hundred self-supporting churches in China. They also contribute largely for Christian schools. In Canton, we have the "Baptist Academy," owning their own school-building and employing their own teachers. All the expenses of the school are borne by the Chinese, independently of the mission. Some of the funds, it is true, come from the Chinese in America, but this does not change the fact that it is an object lesson of Chinese self-help in mission work. Then we have a native tract society, and a native evangelization society who own their own chapel connected with our mission, and a general non-denominational society for loaning books and carrying Christian literature to the neglected parts of the province. We may trust the Chinese to take an active part of the proclamation of the Gospel to their own countrymen, as well as train their children in Christian and general culture. There is, then, every reason to hope for the success of the Gospel in China, whether we look at its Divine origin, at those to whom its propagation has been committed, in the Providence of God, at the Divine Power who is working with us, or the Divine blessing which is promised to accompany God's Word.

When we add to the influence of Christian Healing, Christian Education and Christian Literature, that of Christian Preaching, all must feel that Christianity is the great force to which we must look for the regeneration of China—the chief Reconstructive agency at work leading China in the path of real progress and prosperity.

CHAPTER XVI.

HINDRANCES.

WHILE hopeful of the future and anxious to see China falling into line with the nations of the West in the procession toward improvement, candor compels me to say that all the obstacles to this consummation are not found among the Chinese. In some regards, at least, we nations of the West have ourselves to blame for the slowness which China shows in adopting our ideas of progress. Some of these hindrances are preventable; and all true friends of real progress in the world should seek to remove them. To be fair, we must put ourselves in China's place, and endeavor to view things from a Chinese standpoint; or, better still, place ourselves at a point outside of our little world, and try to view things with the impartiality that we might conceive an angel would, stationed where he could see all the nations of the earth, and judge of all with an equal knowledge.

Let us remember, in the first place, that China did

TOKIO.

not always pursue a policy of exclusion, and that her exclusiveness was due to a great extent to the faults of the men from the West. In the fourteenth and fifteenth centuries, the Polos and others were welcome guests at the Mongol court, and foreign commerce flourished with the ports of Cheh Kiang and Fuk Kien. It was not until after the Portuguese and Spanish explorers had made their expeditions in the sixteenth century, that the opposition to foreigners began. Any one who reads the accounts of Da Gama's atrocities in India may well understand why China should not care to have intercourse with such foreigners. The Portuguese settled in Macao, in 1557, peaceably, and the English stormed the Canton forts in 1737. Commercial intercourse was attempted by Queen Elizabeth ; and Ningpo, Formosa, Amoy and Canton had some foreign trade. Early European trading with pagan nations bore too much resemblance to what we would now call freebooting expeditions for us to wonder why those nations should object to the strangers. It is through such traders that the Chinese got their first impressions of Western nations.

Nor has modern commercial intercourse always been of such a character as to lead the Chinese to have a very great admiration for the morality of a so-called Christian civilization. Whatever those interested in it may think of the morality of the

opium traffic, there is no doubt that the Chinese
look upon it as a bane, and the introduction of the
drug a wrong inflicted upon their country. The so-
called " opium war " is not an event in the history
of his country that any Briton can look upon with
pride, however ready he may be to excuse it. Dr.
Martin,* quotes from a Chinese scholarly gentleman
as follows: " Commencing with the last years of the
Ming dynasty, we opened the seaports of Kwang
Tung to foreign trade, doing a profitable business
in tea and silks, receiving in return fabrics of
woolen and cotton suited to our wants; as well
as clocks, watches, mirrors, and other articles of
luxury. But opium came in at the same time, and
its poisonous streams have penetrated to the core of
the Flowery Land. The blame of this partly rests
upon us, but when we go to the root of the evil, it
is impossible to exculpate the English from the
guilt of originating the traffic."

After giving ample credit to the advantages
gained from foreign intercourse, he sums up by
saying that the " advantages derived from foreign
commerce are not sufficient to make amends for the
evils to which it has given rise. But the benefits
which we derive from the teachings of the missionaries are more than we can enumerate." This is
the way in which the more intelligent among the

* " The Chinese," by Dr. W. A. P. Martin, 1881 (Han Lin Papers).

Chinese look upon the opium trade, and, rightly or wrongly, they regard it as a hindrance to the acceptance of Western ideas.

As to the rest of mankind, probably those best acquainted with the true state of the case, will say with Dr. Martin : " To the renovation of the Chinese people, the most formidable obstacle is the use of opium, a vice of recent growth, for the prevalence of which we have to thank the unscrupulous cupidity of Christian nations."

The *coolie traffic* is another blot on the escutcheon of Western civilization. In this case Great Britain has acted fairly; and it is to the greed of gain on the part of Portuguese, Spanish and American traders and ship-masters that we must ascribe most of the blame. Again, whatever may be our opinion of the morality of the traffic, there is no doubt in the mind of any one acquainted with the subject but that it has tended in a great degree, and justly too, to shake the confidence of the Chinese people in the justice and benevolence of Western nations. In this case, as with regard to opium, they judge unjustly, for they take no account of the public opinion in other lands which oppose these things, but only reason from those with whom they are brought into contact, and the effects of the trade as they see it. And this is perfectly natural. We are apt to judge of a nation by the specimens that we see of that nation, and count the actual facts we know of as an outcome of the morality of the whole nation. Mistaken as these views often are, they no doubt have a powerful influence, especially with a narrow-minded but practical people, unacquainted with the rest of the world.

The *overbearing manners* of so many foreigners create a prejudice against Western civilization. We may associate brusqueness with frankness and open-heartedness, but to the Chinese it is simply rudeness. All their ideas of gentlemanliness are identified with a gentle, suave manner. Insincerity and even duplicity are nothing in their estimation, when compared with impoliteness and want of consideration for the feelings of another. To see men from other lands, who should come and deport themselves as guests, acting as if they were the lords of creation and the whole land belonged to them, gives the Chinese a very poor opinion of our civilization. It is not strange that from their standpoint they regard foreigners as boors and barbarians—men who sacrifice to the god of forces. After this feeling of repulsion wears off they may learn to estimate a foreigner at his true value, as a man of honor and sincerity, but our honest bluntness does not accord with Asiatic notions of culture and refinement. Anglo-Saxons seem never to forget that they belong

to a conquering race; and are but too apt to show
it in their intercourse with others. Though we
may feel that we are really superior to others, yet
to show it without regarding their feelings is sure
to prejudice them against us, and make fear the
only motive why they respect us. Certainly overbearing and aggressive manners do not commend
Western civilization to the Chinese.

The *assumption of superiority and authority*
on the part of foreigners is another thing that the
Chinese dislike, and that tends to prejudice them
against the West. Much of the opposition to
Christian missions had its origin in the assumption
of rank and power on the part of Roman Catholic
bishops and priests, who often hang out lanterns
at their door with Chinese titles of rank painted on
them, and claim to visit native officials as of equal
rank with them. Then they sometimes claim the
right of asylum for their churches, and endeavor
to shield their converts from the civil power. Unjust and unreasonable persecution so often arises
from the heathen that it is not strange that the
priests should endeavor to shelter and protect the
innocent sufferer, and yet the claiming the right—
the claiming an *imperium in imperio*—excites the
jealousy of the authorities. This assumption of authority and rank leads the Chinese authorities to
suspect political motives, and to feel that foreigners

20

are trying to supersede them in their influence over the people.

Protestant missionaries too have been accused of being too ready to have recourse to " the inevitable gun-boat." Of course missionaries are subjects and citizens just as much as merchants and travelers are ; and if protection for them and their interests were withdrawn, the Chinese authorities would soon find an excuse for expelling them altogether. If all the native mandarins would only consent to deal fairly and honorably with missionaries and their converts, as some of them are inclined to do, there would be little need for gun-boats ; but as long as they foment mobs and try to curry favor with the heathen by treating the native Christians as rebels, and the missionaries as pests, they render the protection of foreign Powers necessary to preserve the lives and property of those who are under their care. Let Chinese mandarins but treat Europeans and Americans as fairly as our judges do the Chinese, and there would be no trouble. Still we should always be very slow to appeal to secular authority, and suffer much wrong before feeling compelled to do so. Except where life is in danger it is doubtful whether we should have recourse to war vessels, and even when endangered, we might choose personally to suffer, were it not that the Chinese would feel emboldened by one case of un-

noticed murder to permit or instigate others. The
solidarity of foreigners in China is such, and the
effrontery of the ruling class is such, that one cannot separate himself from the mass without involv-
ing the Cause which is dearer than life. Let the
Chinese authorities but show themselves worthy of
confidence and determined to do what is right, and
missionaries will not object to put themselves in
their power, but as long as men like Chang Chi
Tung are high in authority, we must rely on our
rights as citizens, as Paul did. With the Sung Po
massacre and the subsequent treatment of all concerned in it fresh in their minds, men will be slow
to desire to commit themselves to the tender mercies of plausible but malignant Chinese mandarins.
While the Chinese have themselves to blame almost
entirely for any appeal to force on the part of
Western governments, still missionaries who go
forth as ambassadors of the Prince of Peace should
be slow to avail themselves of any appeal to the
force of arms. There is no doubt whatever that,
with the assumption of rank and the appeal to force
out of the way, the Chinese authorities would be inclined to look more favorably on the missionary
enterprise.

The *freedom of intercourse between the sexes* in
the West is another obstacle in the way of the
Chinese accepting our civilization. They look on

all such freedom as akin to immorality. In all heathen lands and wherever polygamy prevails, woman is looked upon as the mere slave or plaything of the man. The Chinese, who are in this ditch, look upon everything from their own low and muddy standpoint. With their contracted horizon they are unable to understand how women can mingle with men as equals in culture, intelligence, acquaintance with literature and nobility of character. The *status* of woman in China is little in advance of what it was in Egypt and Babylonia centuries before Christ, and the Chinese cannot conceive of her as elevated by Christianity. Their ancient writings condemn all familiarity between the sexes in public; even to touch a woman's hand is an offense. All their training is to look with contempt upon woman as an inferior, and what we call "society" is unknown. The only social intercourse with woman outside of the family is spending an evening in the company of the demi-monde and loose women on a "flower-boat," or in a house of ill-fame. Hence, until their ideas are elevated by Christianity, they cannot understand the morality of an evening spent in conversation and music.

Then, too, the Chinese have very strict ideas as to the modesty of females who are what they should be. The dress of the women is exceedingly modest and becoming; the neck is well covered and the

form is concealed by their loose garments. Some
Chinese who have mingled in society in the capitals
of Europe and America are much scandalized by the
" full dress " of the women, and feel if this is the
outcome of Western civilization they hope the day
will be far distant when it will prevail in China.
Fashions that might be innocuous in the West,
where we have been long used to seeing them, would
be conducive to laxity of morals in a land where the
people are unaccustomed to them. Such costumes
give the Chinese low ideas of the modesty and
morality of the women of the West.

These impressions as to the laxity of foreign
morals are intensified by the stories told by Chinese
emigrants to America and Australia. As these men
reside in the " China-towns " of our cities they get
their ideas from the atmosphere of the slums,—the
scum of European emigrants with whom they are
thrown into daily contact. Hence their notions of
the morality of foreign women get to be very low.
Then, too, the lives of many of the foreigners in the
seaports of China tend to confirm them in their
opinions. As the young men come from the country villages of China, where every man is married, to
the busy haunts of trade on the sea-coast, it is not
strange that they contrast the morality of the quiet
Chinese home with the looseness of morals as to the
relation between the sexes in the European settle-

ments, much to the disadvantage of the foreigner. These things, viewed through the magnifying glass of their own pride of race and self-conceit, tend to make them think that there would be no gain to morality if they should adopt the customs of the men from beyond the sea.

The foregoing remarks may, perhaps, seem uncalled for, but it is impossible to give a true statement of Chinese objections to Western civilization without mentioning them. All who are acquainted with the feeling of the Chinese towards our form of civilization know that this is one of the chief hindrances in the way of their adopting "foreign customs."

As has been mentioned before, there has been a disposition of late years, fostered to some extent by the Government, for the Chinese to study "Western Learning," by which they mean physical science. As a certain class of students in the West arrogate to themselves the name of "Scientists," ignoring all mental and moral science, so the Chinese have the idea that physical research is the only branch that the men of the West think worthy of notice. As morality and sociology lie at the root of Chinese culture, they fancy that they are far in advance of us as regards the true needs of the individual and society. Supposing that Western scholars confine their thoughts to the domain of Nature, it is not

YOKOHAMA.

strange that some of the more thoughtful among the Chinese should look with no little concern upon the prevalence of such ideas in China. Having little sympathy with the spiritual part of the Christian religion, they fail to see how it presents an antidote to materialism. Nor are the fears of these lovers of their country unfounded, if " Western learning " is to be introduced, divorced from moral, mental, and religious culture. We sympathize sincerely with these patriots, and only blame them for not giving us credit for this sympathy, and for their failure to understand that physical science does not exhaust the content of the learning from the West. It is said that when Dr. Legge, Professor of Chinese at Oxford, met the Chinese Minister to England, he asked him what he thought of English civilization. The minister replied : " In material civilization you far surpass us." " But do you not think that our morality is superior too ? " In surprise the Chinese exclaimed : " How can you say, as a candid man, that the morality of England can compare with that of China ! " When those who have visited the West have such impressions, is it strange that the great mass of the Chinese should be slow to adopt our civilization in its entirety ? The men of Western lands must convince the Chinese that we are not mere nations of traders, who care only for dollars and cents, or of materialists who are content with conveniences and luxuries, or of warriors who wish to carry their point by brute force. Until we succeed in doing this, Western civilization will not prove so attractive to China as we would like to see it.

As far as possible we must try and remove these hindrances. The misunderstanding and narrowness of view of the Chinese must be removed by giving them information and making known to them the truth ; their good will must be won by adjusting ourselves to them, not by lowering any standard, but by avoiding all that gives needless offense. Any attempt on the part of Western nations to *impose* our civilization upon them will only tend to delay its adoption. If we make them see that it is desirable, they will, in the course of time, wish, of themselves, to adopt all that is really valuable in our form of of civilization. The surest and shortest way to this end is to lead them to understand and value the Christian religion which is the fountain of all that is good in our civilization.

As to the *time* and *manner* of introducing these changes, we must leave these largely to the Chinese themselves. They naturally move slowly and deliberately, but doubtless events like the present war with Japan will quicken their pace. We find in the history of nations that the great, heavy press of war is often needed to press out the energy and determination which are needed to bring any important enterprise to a conclusion. No nation can afford to lag too far behind in the great march of events which are to usher in the twentieth century. China will feel that she is in the rush and whirl of the stream and must advance or go to the bottom. No doubt she will catch some of the spirit of her neighbor, and will move more rapidly than she has been moving. Periods of re-action like that following the war with France will probably pass over her, but her progress will continue. We must not be too impatient with her, but remember that large masses may have a great momentum, even though they may not move rapidly—that permanent changes, introduced gradually, are of more value than more rapid strides made fitfully. A gentle pressure from without may sometimes be needed to jog her memory and hasten her progress, but it is much better that the impulse come from within if possible.

We must let China introduce changes, too, in her own peculiar manner. It is amusing to see how anxious those advanced minds who advocate changes are to avoid opposition by compounding with conservatism. They feel that they must propitiate the Chinese claim to superiority by a little flattering. They sacrifice truth for policy, in order to gain their ends. Even a man of the intelligence of Prince

Kung, in his memorial for the establishment of a college in Pekin for the cultivation of Western science, says: " As for the imputation of abandoning the methods of China, is it not altogether a fictitious charge? For, on inquiry, it will be found that Western science had its root in the astronomy of China, which Western scholars confess themselves to have derived from Eastern lands. . . In reality the original belonged to China, and the Europeans learned them from us. If, therefore, we apply ourselves to those studies, we will be building on our foundation." He speaks of some who will " denounce the proposal that Chinese must submit to be instructed by the people from the West, as shameful in the extreme."

As Chinese reformers have to contend against this strong conservative, anti-foreign sentiment on the part of many in positions of influence and of the great bulk of the " literates," we must allow them to introduce changes in their own way. We must not be too hard on them for a little desire to keep in the good graces of men that they may in the end carry them along with them. The demands of trade and even a sincere interest in the advancement of China may want to choose their own time and methods, but, so progress is made, let us not be too impatient. It is but right that patriotic Chinese should want to develop the resources of their own

COREA BRIDGE.

country, and utilize what they already have, rather than seek to build up the interests of foreigners who flock to their shores. We must not quarrel with China because she does just what we would wish our own people to do. So she moves, let her do it in her own way. Of course she will have to learn by her own mistakes, as all the rest of us do : then she will see the superiority of what we have to offer her.

Let us, then, in our sincere desire to see China progressing, remove all the stumbling-blocks we can, and encourage her to move forward in the path of reform. If her eyes were not blinded, she would see that moral changes are what she needs most, and that an honest, stalwart Christian character lies at the root of all real progress. Little as she appreciates it, it is for this that Christian missionaries are laboring, and it is this that all true well-wishers of China really desire.

In this brief survey of China in the stage of transition, we have seen some of the causes that retard her onward progress, and some which tend to promote it. Some are external and others are deeply seated ; some but temporary and others more enduring. Every one interested in China's welfare is watching the conflict which is now going, a conflict of more consequence than the severe war she is passing through—a conflict of ideas. " The truth is mighty and will prevail." I have no doubt whose the ultimate victory will be. If China but understands in this, her day of visitation, she will yet take her place in Christendom. With all her vast population, with all her mighty possibilities, with all her rich past and all her capacities for a glorious future, may we not hope that she will have the courage to reform? Then we may look for the *chung-hing*,— the renaissance that the Chinese love to speak of. China, regenerated by the Gospel of the Lord Jesus Christ, is what we hope for and pray for—that she may issue from the fining-pot of transition, purified and fitted for a place among the Christian nations of the earth.